■SCHOLASTIC

Easy Make & Learn Projects

Southwest Indians

BY DONALD M.
AND PATRICIA J

D1411978

NEW YORK • TORONTO • LONDON • AUCKLAND • SYDNEY
MEXICO CITY • NEW DELHI • HONG KONG • BUENOS AIRES

Teaching *Resources*

For my Janine—
She Who Cares for Others

D M S

....

To the travelers from Berengia—
whenever they arrived

P J W

ACKNOWLEDGMENTS

Special thanks to our consultant on this book, Professor Lotsee F. Patterson, Ph.D. (Comanche),
the University of Oklahoma School of Library and Information Studies

Front cover and interior design by Kathy Massaro
Cover photo by Studio 10
Cover and interior artwork by Patricia J. Wynne

ISBN: 0-439-24115-4
Copyright © 2005 by Donald M. Silver and Patricia J. Wynne
Published by Scholastic Inc.
All rights reserved.
Printed in the U.S.A.

1 2 3 4 5 6 7 8 9 10   40   13 12 11 10 09 08 07 06 05

Contents

Introduction

~~~~~

◇ ◇ ◇ ◇

North America was home to millions of people who belonged to hundreds of different tribes when Europeans discovered what was, to them, a new world. More than 1,000 years ago, where New Mexico, Arizona, Utah, and Colorado now meet, Native American peoples such as the Hopi, Zuni, Navajo, and Jicarilla Apache were living in complex societies, raising families, building houses, farming, and creating tools. Before that, the ancestors of these peoples had built homes by carving into the walls of cliffs, and systems of roads so they could trade with one another. This book is about the descendants of these peoples as well as other tribes who moved to the Southwest.

The models, manipulatives, accompanying background information, and lessons in this book will help motivate your students to learn about how various Southwest Indian tribes lived several centuries ago. (NOTE: We use the term *Southwest Indians* to talk broadly about peoples living in the southwest regions of the current United States. In actuality, a wealth of different cultures with different customs, languages, and traditions comprise this group. See Sensitivity to Native Cultures, below, for more.)

Each lesson indicates the specific tribe or tribes whose homes, tools, or cooking methods are depicted. Students will learn about where tribes such as the Mescalero Apache and Navajo lived, about their varied histories and cultures, and the ways in which the different peoples met their needs for shelter, clothing, food, transportation, and communication. They will find out how the use of natural resources varied depending on each group's location. The models and lessons in this book will also help students build content area knowledge, increase their vocabulary, and improve their reading skills.

SENSITIVITY TO NATIVE CULTURES

◈ Believing that he had reached the Indies, the explorer Christopher Columbus called the native inhabitants of the Americas, *Indians*. It is important to point out to students that the name *Indian* was given by outsiders. For tribes such as the Navajo, Hopi, and Zuni, however, their true names are the ones they gave themselves. Today, both the terms American Indians and Native Americans are used to refer to these peoples (also called tribes) as well as their descendants who continue their traditions today. In this book, the terms are used interchangeably. However, whenever possible, specific tribal names are used.*

Since this book focuses mainly on the lives of different Native peoples prior to their contact with European explorers (around the year 1500), the background information and lessons provided refers to them in the past tense. However, it is important to make it clear to your students that Native peoples still live in the United States today, participating in contemporary culture while still preserving their Native traditions.

Explain to students that it is difficult to pinpoint exactly when different tribes built the homes, wore the clothing, and created the other artifacts represented by the models in this book. Information about how Native Americans lived centuries ago comes from stories passed down from one generation of Native Americans to the next about their ancestors' lives and times, from scholarly work by archaeologists and anthropologists, as well as from drawings and written accounts made by early European explorers after they observed aspects of Native American life.

Because the cultures of Native American peoples are so diverse, representing every aspect of life in each tribe is beyond the scope of this book. However, it was common for different groups to use variations of many items, such as baskets and pottery. Each lesson identifies the specific tribe or tribes whose homes, clothing, and tools are depicted. However, it is probable that other tribes used similar items as well.

The artist created the illustrations in this book in the style of centuries-old artifacts from specific Native American tribes. After making careful observations of actual artifacts, the artist made every effort to represent them accurately, though more simply, in the models that follow. Note however that the designs depicted on the illustrations of pottery and baskets are based on nineteenth century Native American artifacts.

Models representing structures such as buildings and techniques for making pottery, baskets, and tools date back to before Native Americans living in the Southwest came into contact with Spanish explorers. However, some of the models do reflect the influence of the Spanish, who arrived around 1540. For example, From Sheep to Blanket (page 75) reflects the introduction of domesticated sheep to the region by the Spanish.

Native American cultures hold deep spiritual beliefs. Certain topics, such as their use of feathers, face masks, and Kachina dolls, hold a significance much deeper for Native Americans than for those who do not share their heritage or beliefs. For this reason, you may not find in this book the lessons and activities typically found in books for students about Native Americans because we have tried to omit any topics that hold deep spiritual significance for these peoples. Please impress upon your students that the models and activities in this book are intended for them to learn about and respect the unique and varied cultures of Native Americans.

---

* For more on this subject, see "Native American Indian Studies: A Note on Names" (http://www.umass.edu/legal/derrico/name.html) by Peter d'Errico, the president of NativeWeb (http://www.nativeweb.org), a Web site that provides resources about indigenous peoples around the world.

What's Inside

The models and manipulatives in this book are designed to teach your students about the daily life of different Southwest Indian peoples who lived several centuries ago. Each lesson contains the following sections:

MODEL ILLUSTRATION

This picture, labeled with the model name, shows how the finished model looks. It can be helpful to use as a reference when making the model.

NATIVE TRADITIONS

Background information on the topic appears in this section. Depending on the level of your students, you may use some or all of this information with the Teaching With the Model section.

MAKING THE MODEL

These easy-to-follow instructions include diagrams for assembling the models. See the Helpful Hints for Model-Making section, page 7, for guidance in following the instructions.

TEACHING WITH THE MODEL

This section is a step-by-step lesson map with discussion questions. The questions use the models and background information to teach the topic's main concepts.

DO MORE

In this section, you'll find related activities to extend your students' investigation of the topic.

Connections to the Social Studies Standards

The lessons in this book connect to the social studies standards outlined by The National Council for the Social Studies (NCSS)—the organization that offers recommendations for the teaching of social studies in this country.

The lessons also correlate with history standards outlined by Mid-Continent Regional Educational Laboratory (McRel), an organization that collects and synthesizes national and state K–12 standards.

NCSS STANDARDS

Culture

◆ Explore and compare ways different cultures meet human needs and concerns.

◆ Compare ways people in different cultures interact with their physical environment.

Time, Continuity & Change

◆ Use various sources, such as maps, to learn about the past.

◆ Compare and contrast accounts about the past to identify ways they help us understand the past.

People, Places & Environments

◆ Describe how climate and seasonal changes affect the people in different environments.

◆ Identify ways people create places, such as their use of land and homes, that reflect their culture, wants, and needs.

McREL STANDARDS

◆ Knows geographical settings, food, clothing, homes, crafts, and rituals of Native American societies long ago.

◆ Knows that people communicated with each other in the past through pictographs.

◆ Knows the ways that families long ago expressed and transmitted their beliefs and values through, for example, oral tradition, food, language, and arts and crafts.

Sources: *Curriculum Standards for Social Studies: Expectations of Excellence* © 1994 the National Council for the Social Studies.

Content Knowledge: A Compendium of Standards and Benchmarks for K–12 Education (4ᵗʰ ed.). Mid-Continent Research for Education and Learning, 2004.

Helpful Hints for Model-Making

- ❖ If possible, enlarge the pattern pages to make the models easier for students to assemble.

- ❖ The thickest black lines on the reproducible pages are CUT lines.

- ❖ Dotted lines on the reproducible pages are FOLD lines. When folding, be sure to crease well.

- ❖ Some models have slits or windows to cut out. An easy way to make these cuts is to fold the paper at a right angle to the solid cut lines. Then snip along the lines from the crease of the fold inward.

- ❖ Often glue sticks can be substituted for tape. Some situations, such as creating flaps, will require tape.

- ❖ If students will be coloring and taping the models, have them color first so they won't have to color over the tape.

- ❖ Some models are more challenging to assemble than others. Read through each Making the Model section (or make the model yourself) beforehand to determine if it's appropriate for your students to do on their own. You can make a more challenging model yourself and use it as a classroom demonstration tool.

- ❖ If a single model will be handled a great deal, use heavier paper to create it. Either photocopy the reproducible patterns onto heavyweight paper or glue them onto construction paper before beginning assembly.

Model Coloring Tips

If students wish to color the models, point out that Native Americans used natural materials from plants, animals, rocks, and soil to build their homes, make their clothes, and so on. Students can use different shades of the colors described here to color their models.

deerskin: tan
wood: light brown
earthen floor in hogan, tipi, or wickiup: terra-cotta or ocher
adobe pueblos: yellow-ocher or pale red
pottery: terra-cotta with painted designs that can be white, black, and red
cactus: pale green
cactus fibers for tongs: gray
corn husks and corn: yellow
straw: yellow-ocher
cooked agave: gray
baskets: brown
Hopi clothing and Navajo blanket: black, white, tan, yellow, pale red, indigo, and green

Materials were colored using natural dyes from plants—for example, yellow was made from rabbit weed; black from burnt wood; blue from wild indigo plants; green from sage and fresh grasses; brown from clay; and red from cactus fruits and yucca roots. In addition, Indians in the Southwest cultivated naturally-pigmented cotton plants that grew in a variety of colors, such as rose, rust, brown, mauve, pale green, and light yellow.

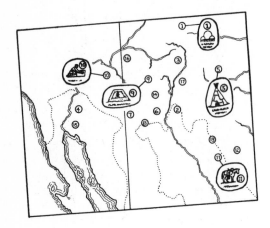

Southwest Indian Tribal Map

〰〰〰
◇ ◇ ◇ ◇

Students make a map showing where tribes of Southwest Indians lived around the year 1500.

NATIVE TRADITIONS

More than 40 tribes lived in the Southwest before Spanish explorers arrived in the region in the sixteenth century. Among them were the Navajo, Apache (including the Mescalero, Jicarilla, and Western Apache), and the Pueblo (including the Hopi, Zuni, and Rio Grande Pueblo tribes). Some groups, such as the Pueblo tribes descended from Native Americans who migrated from Asia between 10,000 and 20,000 years ago. Other tribes, such as the Navajo and Apache, may have come to the region from the subarctic region of present-day Canada and Alaska about 1,000 years ago.

The tribes lived mostly in what is now Arizona and New Mexico, and in parts of Texas, Colorado, Utah, Baja California, and northern Mexico. Their homes were in the valleys of the Rio Grande and the Colorado River, the Chihuahuan and Sonoran deserts, and the mountains and flat-topped mesas that make up the landscape of the Southwest. This region was, and is, dry most of the year. When rain comes, it can be heavy enough to cause flash floods.

The map students assemble in this lesson depicts approximate pre-contact locations of the different tribes around 1500. These locations are based on information passed down through Native American oral traditions and archaeological evidence.

MAKING THE MODEL

1 Direct students to cut out the two halves of the map and tape them together. To make the map sturdier, they can attach it to a piece of cardboard or construction paper.

2 Have students cut out the 17 pieces on page 12 and then match the number on each piece to the corresponding number on the map.

3 Students should tape or glue each picture near its number and then draw a line from the picture to the number. They can then color the map as desired.

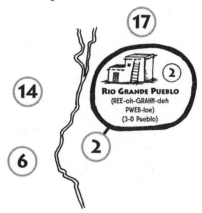

RIO GRANDE PUEBLO
(REE-oh-GRAHN-deh
PWEB-loe)
(3-D Pueblo)

Do More!

TEACHING WITH THE MODEL

1 Explain to students that the pieces they taped to the map correspond to the models they will be making. Each piece depicts a model and indicates the tribe or tribes to which it relates. Ask students to locate on their maps the Pacific Ocean, the Gulf of California, the Colorado River and the Rio Grande before answering the questions below.

❖ What are the names of some of the Southwest Indian tribes? (*Navajo, Apache [including the Mescalero, Jicarilla, and Western Apache], and the Pueblo [including the Hopi, Zuni, and Rio Grande Pueblo tribes]*)

❖ How would you describe the physical features of the region? (*It has rivers, valleys, mountains, deserts, and mesas. It's dry most of the year.*)

❖ When did Native Americans arrive in the Southwest? (*Some tribes reached the region between 10,000 and 20,000 years ago. Others, such as the Apache and Navajo, arrived about 1,000 years ago.*)

Make two photocopies of the political map on page 13 for each student. (Enlarge the maps, if possible.) On one of the political maps, challenge students to write the modern-day names of each state. (They can use the states' two-letter postal codes.) Then, using their tribal map as a guide, have them note on the political map where different Southwestern Indian tribes lived before the arrival of Europeans to this region.

Where do these tribes live today? Help students research where the majority of the people in these tribes currently live and record the name of each tribe or group of tribes on the second map. (See page 80 for a list of resources students can use for their research.)

Compare the two maps. What can students generalize about the differences and similarities in the maps?

SOUTHWEST INDIAN TRIBAL MAP
(AROUND 1500)

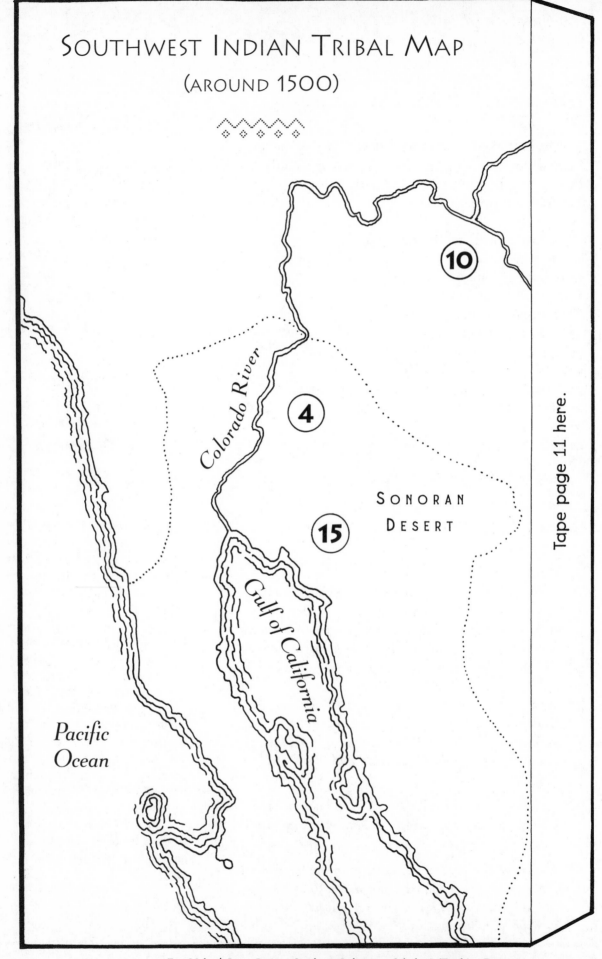

10

4

Colorado River

SONORAN DESERT

15

Gulf of California

Pacific Ocean

Tape page 11 here.

10

Easy Make & Learn Projects: Southwest Indians   Scholastic Teaching Resources

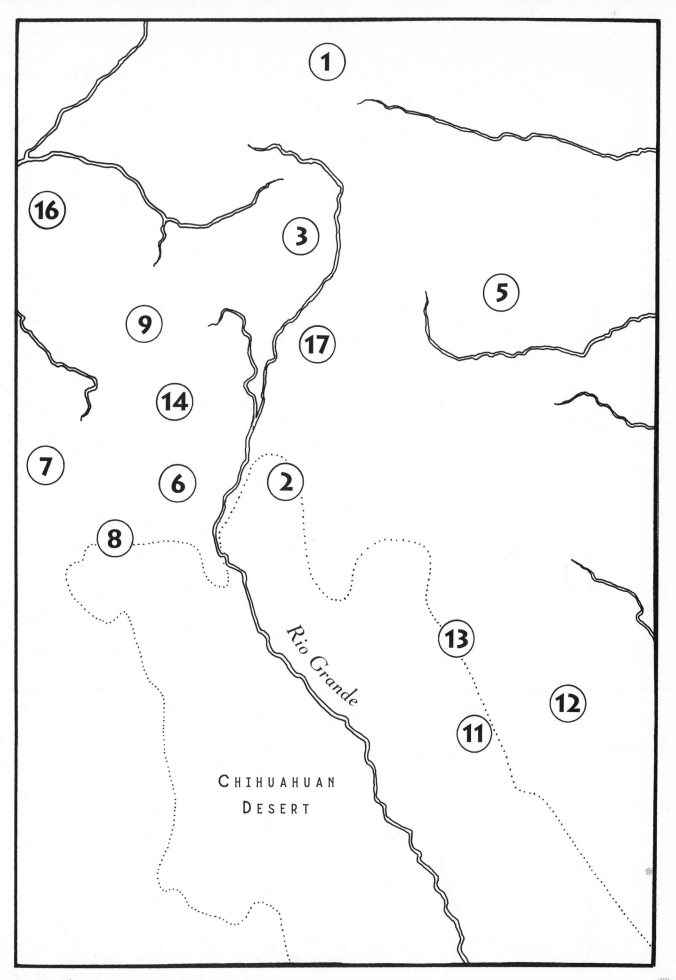

Rio Grande

CHIHUAHUAN
DESERT

SOUTHWEST INDIAN TRIBAL MAP

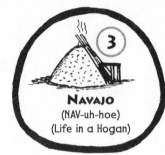

SOUTHWEST INDIAN ANCESTORS 1
(Say It With Pictures)

NAVAJO 3
(NAV-uh-hoe)
(Life in a Hogan)

ZUNI 9
(Growing Corn Fold-Up Book)

JICARILLA APACHE 5
(hek-a-REH-ya)
(Life in a Tipi)

HOPI (HOE-pee)
ZUNI (ZOO-nee) 6
(Cactus Fruit Tongs)

WESTERN APACHE/ JICARILLA APACHE 15
(Weave a Basket)

HOPI ZUNI 8
(Finding Food Diorama)

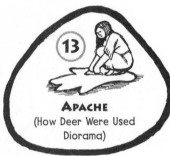

APACHE 13
(How Deer Were Used Diorama)

HOPI 10
(Cooking With Corn Storyboard)

HOPI 16
(Who Wore What? Double Diorama)

MESCALERO APACHE 12
(A Roasted Desert Dish)

HOPI ZUNI 7
(Hunter's Throwing Stick)

ZUNI 14
(Painted Pottery)

RIO GRANDE PUEBLO 2
(REE-oh-GRAHN-deh PWEB-loe)
(3-D Pueblo)

MESCALERO APACHE 11
(mehs-cah-LAHR-oh)
(On the Move)

NAVAJO 17
(From Sheep to Blanket)

WESTERN APACHE 4
(uh-PATCH-ee)
(Life in a Wickiup)

Easy Make & Learn Projects: Southwest Indians   Scholastic Teaching Resources

Southwest United States and Mexico

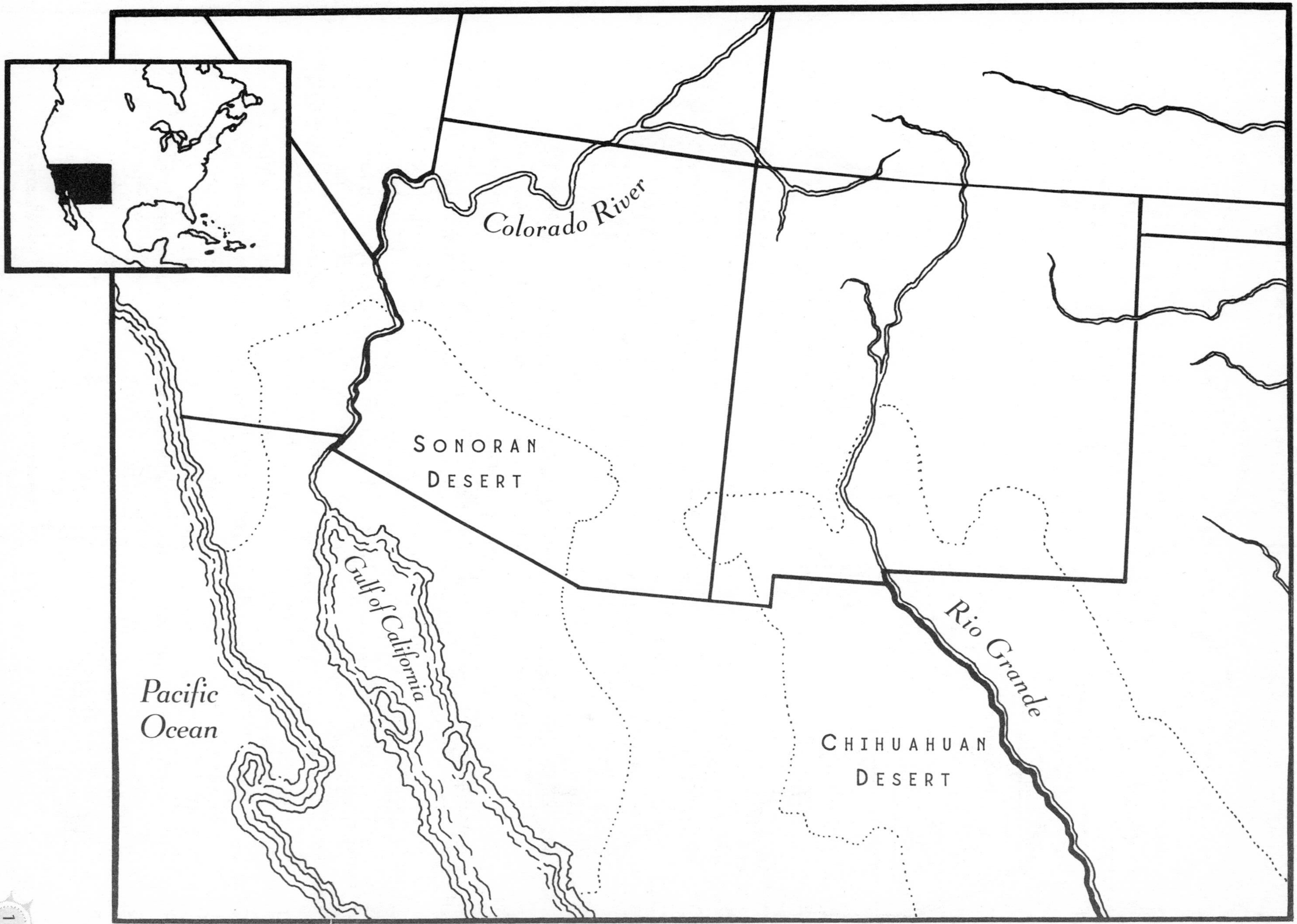

Rio Grande

Chihuahuan Desert

Colorado River

Sonoran Desert

Gulf of California

Pacific Ocean

Say It With Pictures

(SOUTHWEST INDIAN ANCESTORS)

Students make a pictograph dictionary
to learn how prehistoric Native Americans living
in the Southwest used pictures to communicate.

NATIVE TRADITIONS

The Native American tribes of the Southwest didn't have written languages based on an alphabet. They spoke different languages and communicated with other tribes in ways other than written words. The Apache tribes, for instance, conversed in sign language. The Hopi and other Pueblo Indians communicated information by painting pictures called *pictographs*. They also engraved pictures called *petroglyphs* on cave rocks and cliff dwellings using stone chisels.

Many of the pictures, such as the ones redrawn for the model, have been found at ancient Anasazi ruins and date back thousands of years. The Anasazi people, who lived about 7,000 years ago, were the ancestors of the Pueblo Indians.

The pictographs shown on the model in this lesson date back thousands of years to when the ancestors of Southwest Indians lived. They appear to depict handprints, figures of birds and other animals, figures of people, and so on. Although no one really knows the exact meaning of each pictograph, people who have studied them have made educated guesses about their meanings. Some probably had religious or spiritual significance and were important for telling stories, describing the proper way of conducting ceremonies, and recording events. Many contemporary Pueblo artisans still use these motifs in patterns on pottery and tiles.

MAKING THE MODEL

1 Invite students to color the pictures on page 16 as desired and then cut out the four panels.

2 Have students tape the panels in alphabetical order, end to end, as shown.

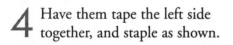

3 Show them how to fold the pages like an accordion so that the title appears on top and page 11 is at the back.

4 Have them tape the left side together, and staple as shown.

TEACHING WITH THE MODEL

1 Ask students to look at each picture and label. Do they think the word matches the image? If not, what word would they choose?

2 How did the Indians of the Southwest communicate with each other? (*The tribes spoke their own languages but had no written languages. To communicate with other tribes, they used various methods. The Apache used sign language; the Hopi and other Pueblo peoples drew pictures.*)

3 What is a pictograph? What is a petroglyph? (*A pictograph is a painted picture. A petroglyph is a picture engraved in stone.*)

4 Point out that the pictures in the dictionary were found at ancient ruins. What might have been the importance of such pictures to the people who created them? (*No one really knows, but the pictures may have been used to record events, tell stories, or convey information about ceremonies.*)

5 Extend the activity by inviting students to create their own pictographs that reflect their environment.

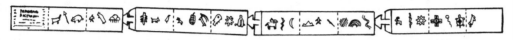

Materials

* photocopy of page 16 for each student
* scissors
* tape or glue sticks
* stapler
* crayons, colored pencils or markers (optional)

Do More!

Challenge students to find examples of petroglyphs from the Southwest in the library or on the Internet. Suggest that they explore Web sites for places such as the Petroglyph National Monument in Albuquerque, New Mexico (www.nps.gov/petr/), or Seminole Canyon State Park, near Comstock, Texas (www.tpwd.state.tx.us/park/seminole/). Hold a class discussion about the examples that students found; talk about what the symbols might mean and how they are similar and different. (Always supervise students' use of the Internet.)

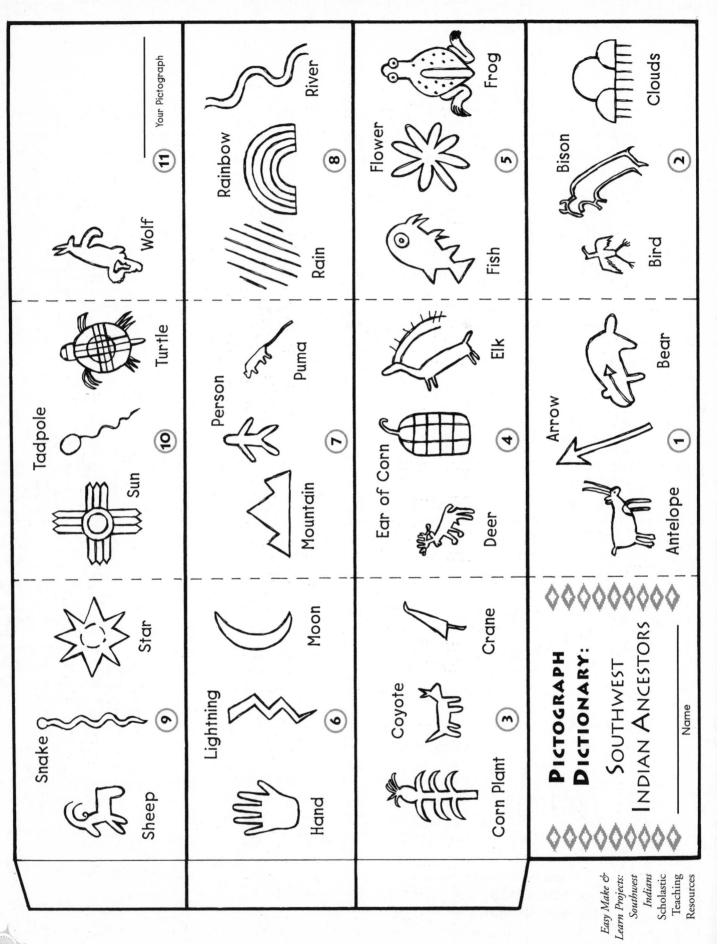

Sheep · Snake · (9) · Star · Tadpole · Sun · (10) · Turtle · Wolf · (11) · Your Pictograph

Hand · Lightning · (6) · Mountain · Person · Puma · (7) · Rain · Rainbow · (8) · River

Corn Plant · Coyote · (3) · Deer · Ear of Corn · Elk · (4) · Fish · Flower · (5) · Frog

Crane · Moon

PICTOGRAPH DICTIONARY: SOUTHWEST INDIAN ANCESTORS

Name

Antelope · (1) · Arrow · Bear · (2) · Bird · Bison · Clouds

Easy Make & Learn Projects: Southwest Indians Scholastic Teaching Resources

3-D Pueblo

(RIO GRANDE PUEBLO)

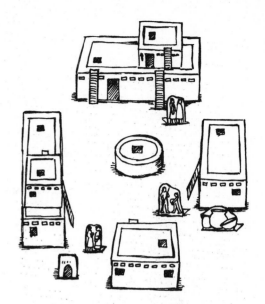

Students make a model that depicts the kind of village that Pueblo Indians lived in around 1300.

NATIVE TRADITIONS

When the first Spanish explorers arrived in the 1500s, they saw clusters of adobe houses built by Indian tribes who lived along the Rio Grande. The Spaniards called these communities *pueblos* (*pueblo* means "village" in Spanish), and the tribes in these villages became known as the Pueblo Indians. Today we refer to the Eastern Pueblo (the Rio Grande tribes such as the Cochiti [ko-CHEE-tee] and the Isleta [ees-LAY-hah]) and the Western Pueblo (the Hopi and the Zuni). The model in this lesson depicts the kind of pueblo that tribes along the Rio Grande lived in around 1300.

The pueblos were similar to today's apartment house complexes situated around public squares or plazas. Constructed of stone or sun-dried adobe bricks, the structures were covered with a plaster of mud. Water from the Rio Grande, so important to these tribes, made it possible to use these materials for building. The pueblo houses were from two to six stories high, and the walls, with openings to let in light, were often several feet thick. Each house had a flat roof, made of pieces of pine or aspen, supported by wooden beams which were covered with a mixture of mud and grass, and brush.

More than one family lived in a pueblo dwelling, but they were all part of a clan—people related through the women in the family. When a man married, he moved into his wife's pueblo home, which belonged to all the women living in it.

When a home grew crowded, more rooms or stories were added. In the latter case, a part of the roof of one story became the terrace for the people living above it. Families used rooftop terraces for a variety of activities, such as processing hides, drying corn and chilies, and for eating and sleeping in summer. People reached each level in a multi-storied building using a ladder. For security, they removed the ladders at night or if the village was under attack.

Within a dwelling, families had separate rooms for living and storing dried corn and other foods. In some houses, the bottom story was used entirely for storage. During the day, wooden poles suspended from the ceiling stored bedding. At mealtime, families would sit on rolled blankets around a pot of food that was cooked on a center-floor hearth.

Rooftop terraces had chimneys made of broken pottery and mortar which drew smoke out of the rooms. Families also baked and roasted food in outdoor ovens made of stone and adobe bricks. These could be found in the plazas or on rooftops.

The houses were built around squares or plazas. In each village, the men also built circular rooms called *kivas* (KEE-vaz). Most kivas were built underground, but some were sunk halfway underground, while others were constructed completely above ground. Kivas were the men's domain. They descended ladders to enter these chambers, where they held meetings and performed religious ceremonies.

Materials

- photocopies of pages 20–22 (enlarge, if possible)
- scissors
- tape
- 8 1/2- by 11-inch sheets of cardboard

OPTIONAL:

- 8 1/2- by 11-inch sheets of sandpaper or tan construction paper
- crayons, colored pencils, or markers (optional)

MAKING THE MODEL

To create this model, divide the class into small groups and have the students in each group assemble their own set of buildings and accessories. Guide students in following these directions to make their models:

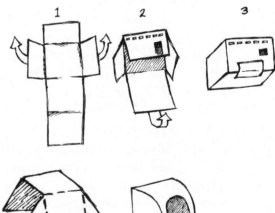

1 Color pages 20–22 as desired. Then cut out the BUILDING patterns along the outer solid lines.

2 For each BUILDING, fold down the sides along the dotted lines. Then fold the floor underneath, and tape as shown.

3 Cut out the OVEN, fold it, and tape as shown.

4 Cut out the KIVA. Form a circle with the base of the KIVA by taping the ends together as shown. Then fold in the flap on the top and tape.

5 Create part of a Pueblo village on the cardboard. (Optional: First tape sandpaper or construction paper to the cardboard.) Position the large and medium BUILDINGS to create a plaza. Add smaller ones on top.

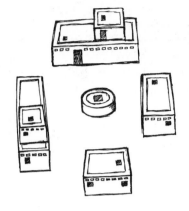

6 Place the KIVA in the middle of the plaza, with space around it.

7 Cut out the LADDERS, PEOPLE, and POTTERY. Fold back the flaps on the PEOPLE and POTTERY and then position the pieces as desired within the Pueblo village. Tape the tops of the LADDERS to the BUILDINGS. Cut out and set aside the CORNFIELD PLOT for the Do More activity, right.

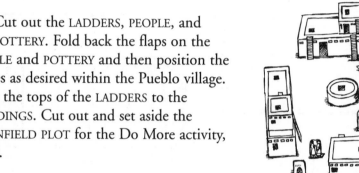

Do More!

Have students create a large Pueblo village by combining their models. They can make multiple plazas and for background settings, draw pictures of rocky cliffs or mesas. Then have students place the CORNFIELD PLOTS outside the walls of their village to show where Rio Grande Pueblo Indians planted their crops.

TEACHING WITH THE MODEL

1 What does this model show? (*It shows the kind of pueblo that different Rio Grande Pueblo tribes lived in around 1300. A pueblo is a village consisting of buildings made of adobe bricks that have been plastered with mud.* Pueblo *is also the Spanish word for "village."*)

2 How were pueblos like apartment house complexes? (*They were two to six stories high. More than one family lived in each building, and additional rooms and stories were added as necessary.*)

3 Why did pueblos have ladders? (*People needed ladders to reach the upper floors of the houses. Ladders could be removed at night or if a village was attacked.*)

4 What was a square or a plaza? (*It was the space around which the houses of a village were built.*)

5 Challenge students to describe what took place inside and outside the houses. (*People lived and worked in the houses and stored corn and other foods there. On rooftop terraces they dried corn, processed hides, and baked and roasted foods in outdoor ovens. In warm weather, they ate and slept on these terraces. Men often conducted meetings and held ceremonies in the kivas.*)

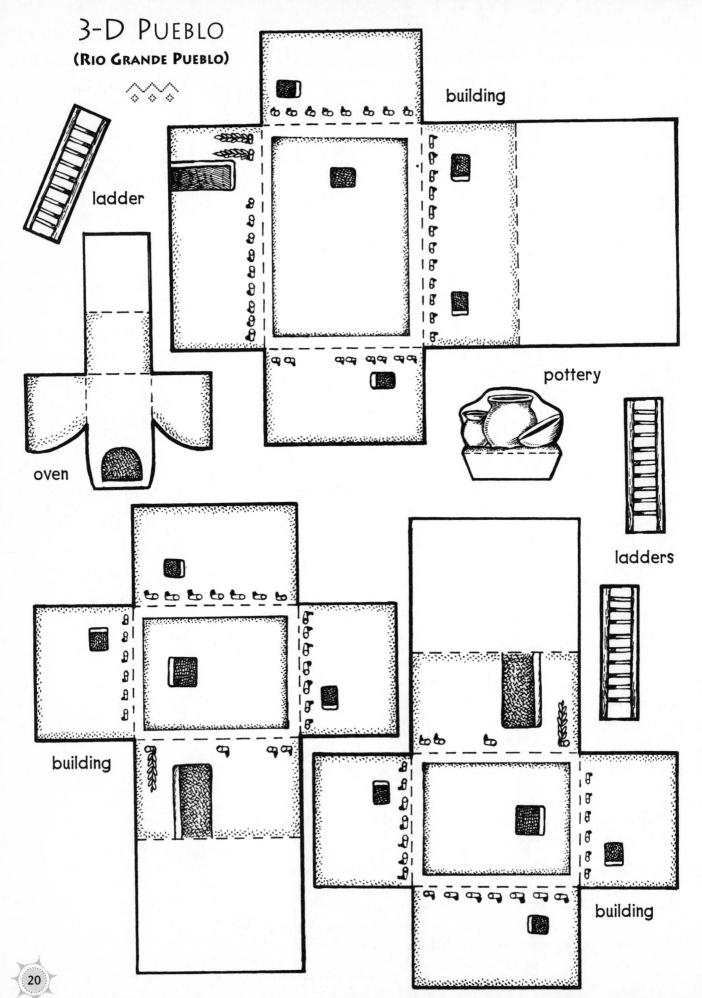

3-D Pueblo
(Rio Grande Pueblo)

ladder

oven

building

pottery

ladders

building

building

Easy Make & Learn Projects: Southwest Indians   Scholastic Teaching Resources

building

ladders

people

building

3-D PUEBLO
(RIO GRANDE PUEBLO)

building

ladder

people

kiva

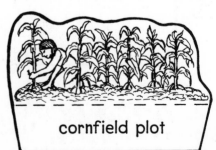

cornfield plot

Easy Make & Learn Projects: Southwest Indians   Scholastic Teaching Resources

Life in a Hogan

(NAVAJO)

Students make a model
of a Navajo house
called a hogan.

NATIVE TRADITIONS

Considered a separate and distinct tribe from their Apache cousins, the Navajo came from the north about 1,000 years ago and settled throughout what is today northern New Mexico. They call themselves the *Dinéh* (dee-NAY), which means "the People."

The Navajo made their living by hunting, farming beans, corn, and squash, and later by raising sheep and other livestock. Unlike their pueblo-dwelling neighbors, they lived in *hogans* (HOE-gahns), meaning "home place."

The earliest hogans were conical in shape and were built from a frame of wooden poles and tree limbs that were covered with bark and mud for insulation and waterproofing. Later hogans, often hexagonal in shape, were built of logs plastered with mud. A hogan had a porch-like entry that faced east, in the direction of the rising sun. An overhang provided shade from the daytime heat.

Inside there was one room without dividing walls or windows. A roof hole allowed smoke from the centrally located fire to escape. Women kept household items such as food and dishes on one side of the room while men stored their hunting tools such as bows and arrows on the other. Women might have kept a wooden loom for weaving inside the hogan, but otherwise there was next to no furniture. A Navajo family would sit on deerskins around the central fire and sleep around it, too.

After the arrival of the Spanish, the Navajo also herded sheep and had to seek grazing lands for the animals. Often a family would build a second hogan near where their sheep grazed. Navajo homes and livestock were owned by the women and were inherited by daughters. A Navajo village was composed of a number of hogans, a sheep corral, dugouts for storage, and gardens for growing corn, beans, and squash.

Materials

- photocopies of pages 26–28 for each student
- scissors
- tape
- crayons, colored pencils, or markers (optional)

MAKING THE MODEL

Guide students in following these directions to make the model:

1 Cut out the GROUND, OUTER HOGAN, INNER HOGAN, and SUPPORT POLES patterns on pages 26–28. Color if desired. Be sure to cut open the flap on the porch-like structure.

2 Cut the slits in the GROUND. Align the opening in the OUTER HOGAN with the entryway on the GROUND. Then insert each of the flaps on the OUTER HOGAN into the slits and tape underneath.

3 Wrap the INNER HOGAN as shown. Then insert it, illustrated side facing in, through the entryway. The INNER HOGAN forms the inside walls.

4 Tape the left-hand side of the porch-like structure to the HOGAN opening to make a cone shape, as shown.

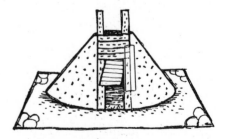

5 Lift up the flap on the porch-like structure. Fold the SUPPORT POLES pattern in half lengthwise. Then center the SUPPORT POLES on the underside of the flap and tape to the edge. Tuck the ends of the SUPPORT POLES into the doorway to secure.

6 Cut out the remaining model pieces. Fold back the flap on the FIRE. Tape it to the STICKS so it stands up. Then place the FIRE inside the hogan, in the center. Also place the RUG inside.

7 Fold back the flaps on the other pieces and tape outside the hogan, as desired.

Ask students to compare their hogan models to their models of the Pueblo village (see page 17). Then, after you study the housing styles of some of the Apache tribes (see page 29), include a comparison to a Western Apache *wickiup* and Jicarilla Apache *tipi*. Ask: "Which structure is most like a hogan? Why do you think so?"

TEACHING WITH THE MODEL

1 Who are the Navajo? (*The Navajo are Native Americans who came from the north and are related to the Apache.*)

2 How did the Navajo make a living? (*They hunted, farmed, and later, after the Spanish arrived, raised sheep.*)

3 What is a hogan? (*A hogan is a one-room Navajo house built in the shape of a cone and constructed from wooden poles and tree limbs, then covered with bark and mud.*)

4 Have students make a Navajo village by placing their hogans together.

LIFE IN A HOGAN (NAVAJO)

ground

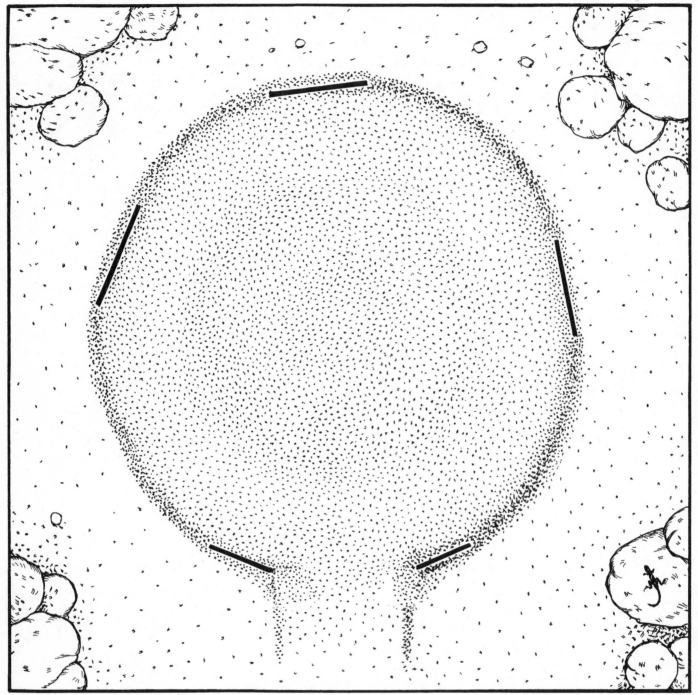

Easy Make & Learn Projects: Southwest Indians · Scholastic Teaching Resources

hunter
making
arrows

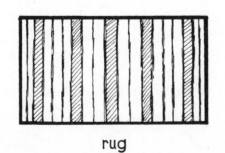

rug

woman
and child
sewing

26

LIFE IN A HOGAN (NAVAJO)

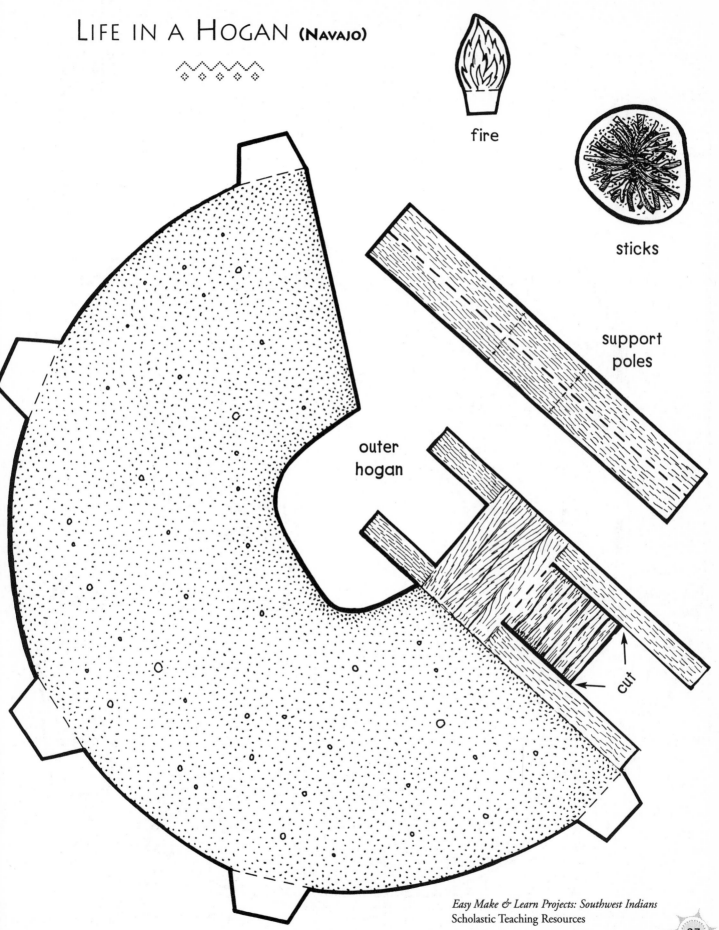

fire

sticks

support poles

outer hogan

cut

Easy Make & Learn Projects: Southwest Indians
Scholastic Teaching Resources

LIFE IN A HOGAN (NAVAJO)

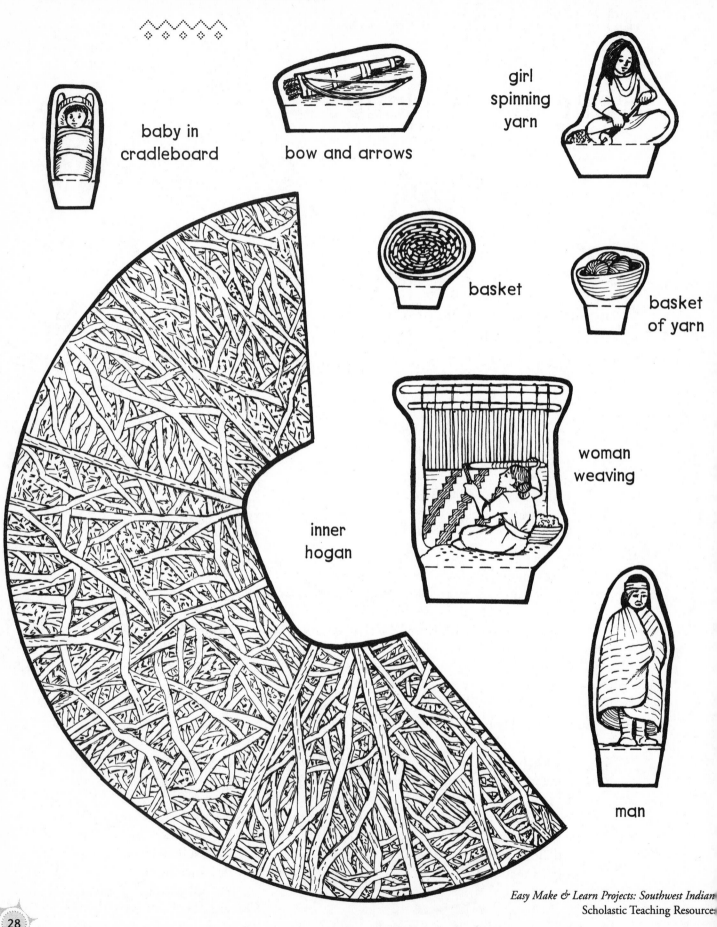

baby in
cradleboard

bow and arrows

girl
spinning
yarn

basket

basket
of yarn

inner
hogan

woman
weaving

man

Life in a Wickiup

(WESTERN APACHE)

and a Tipi

(JICARILLA APACHE)

Students make models of a wickiup
and a tipi and learn how
different groups of Apache lived.

NATIVE TRADITIONS

Sometime between 1200 and 1400, the Apache, like their Navajo
cousins, moved down from the subarctic regions of Alaska and
Canada to the Southwest. The Jicarilla (hek-a-REH-ya), Chiricahua
(chir-ih-KAH-wah), Lipan (LEE-pahn), and Mescalero (mehs-cah-LAHR-oh)
Apache moved into the eastern and southern parts of this region. The
western part became home to a number of tribes, collectively known as the
Western Apache.

The Apache were hunters and gatherers who spoke a common language.
The Western Apache learned how to plant crops from the neighboring
Pueblo Indian tribes, while tribes such as the Jicarilla continued to hunt
buffalo on the Great Plains. Tribes such as the Western Apache, who lived in
the forested mountains of the Southwest, built dome-shaped *wickiups*
(WIK-ee-ups) for shelter. The Jicarilla lived in *tipis* (TEE-pees).

Western Apache women built wickiups out of a framework of poles and
tree limbs that were tied together. In summer, they covered the frame with
thatching made of dried plant materials, such as rushes, yucca leaves, and
grass that they wove together. A fire was built outside the structure. In

winter, they stretched animal hides over the frame, especially on the side where the wind blew. Their fires were then built inside on the earthen floor. An opening at the top allowed smoke to escape. Each wickiup had a doorway that could be closed with a blanket or an animal skin.

The Jicarilla Apache built cone-shaped tipis from a framework of poles cut from trees. Three or more poles (usually an odd number) served as a frame, which was covered with buffalo hides. The hides were sewn together with smoke flaps at the top and closeable flaps at the entrance. Both wickiups and tipis were easily taken down and transported as people moved from place to place.

Materials

- photocopies of pages 33–34 for each student
- scissors
- tape
- crayons, colored pencils, or markers (optional)

MAKING THE MODELS

❊ Wickiup ❊

Guide students in following these directions to make the model:

1 Color pages 33–34 as desired. Then cut out the GROUND pattern on page 33.

2 Cut out the three POLES on page 33. Fold each in half lengthwise along the dotted line and then fold in the ends as shown.

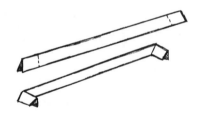

3 Tape the flap at the end of one POLE to one of the spaces indicated on the GROUND. Tape the other end directly opposite. Repeat with the other two POLES to make a frame, as shown at right.

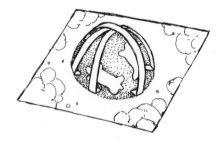

4 Cut out the OUTER WICKIUP on page 34. Tape each tab behind the strip beside it to form a dome shape.

reverse side

tape

30

5 Place the OUTER WICKIUP over the frame.

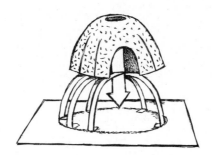

6 Cut out the remaining model pieces on page 34. Fold back the flap on the FIRE. Tape it to the STICKS so it stands up. Then place the FIRE inside the wickiup, in the center.

7 Fold back the flaps on the WOMAN WEAVING BASKET and WILLOW-BRANCH WATER JAR, and tape them around outside the wickiup, as desired. Lean the BABY IN CRADLEBOARD against the wickiup.

Tipi

Guide students in following these directions to make the model:

1 Color pages 35–37 as desired. Cut out the GROUND pattern on page 35.

2 Cut out the five POLES on page 35. Fold each in half lengthwise along the dotted line and then fold in one end on each as shown.

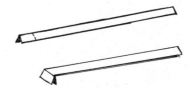

3 Tape the flap at the end of each POLE to one of the spaces indicated on the GROUND.

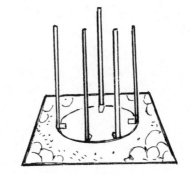

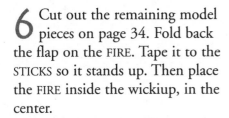

Materials

☼ photocopies of pages 35–37 for each student

☼ scissors

☼ tape

OPTIONAL:

☼ pieces of cardboard, approximately 7 by 7 inches each

☼ crayons, colored pencils, or markers

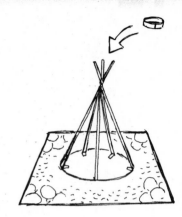

4 Cut out the RAWHIDE TIE on page 36. Form it into a nickel-size ring and tape closed. Gather the tops of the POLES and place the ring over the POLES to hold them together.

5 Cut out the OUTER TIPI on page 36, curve into a cone shape, and tape.

6 Place the OUTER TIPI over the POLES.

7 Cut out the PEOPLE, DOG, BASKETS, SADDLEBAGS, STICKS, and FIRE on page 37. Fold back the flap on the FIRE and tape it to the STICKS so it stands up. Then place the FIRE inside the tipi, in the center.

8 Fold back the flaps on the other pieces and tape or place them outside, as desired.

TEACHING WITH THE MODELS

1 Where did the Apache live? (*Some tribes such as the Jicarilla lived in the eastern and southern parts of the Southwest. The Western Apache lived in the western parts of the region.*)

2 What is a wickiup? (*A wickiup is a dome-shaped house built by tribes such as the Western Apache who lived in the mountains.*)

3 What is a tipi? (*A tipi is a cone-shaped house built by tribes such as the Jicarilla Apache who hunted on the plains.*)

4 Ask students to compare their wickiups and tipis. Challenge them to use their models to explain how each type of house was constructed. (*Answers will vary.*)

5 Why was it important for wickiups and tipis to be easily erected and taken down? (*When Apache tribes moved from place to place, they could take their homes with them.*)

Do More!

Have students put their models together to form a Jicarilla tipi or Western Apache wickiup village. Encourage them to do more research on the Western Apache and the Jicarilla so they can describe what life would have been like in each community.

LIFE IN A WICKIUP (WESTERN APACHE) AND A TIPI (JICARILLA APACHE)

ground (wickiup)

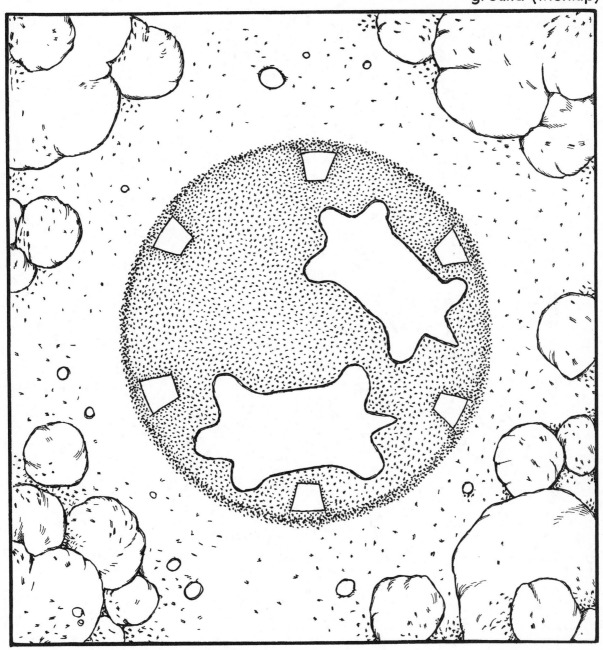

poles (wickiup)

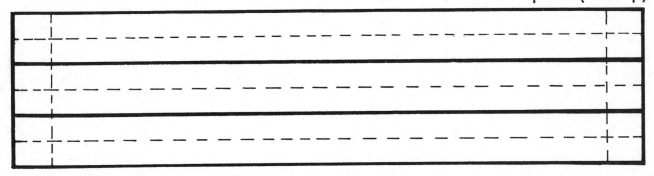

LIFE IN A WICKIUP (WESTERN APACHE) AND A TIPI (JICARILLA APACHE)

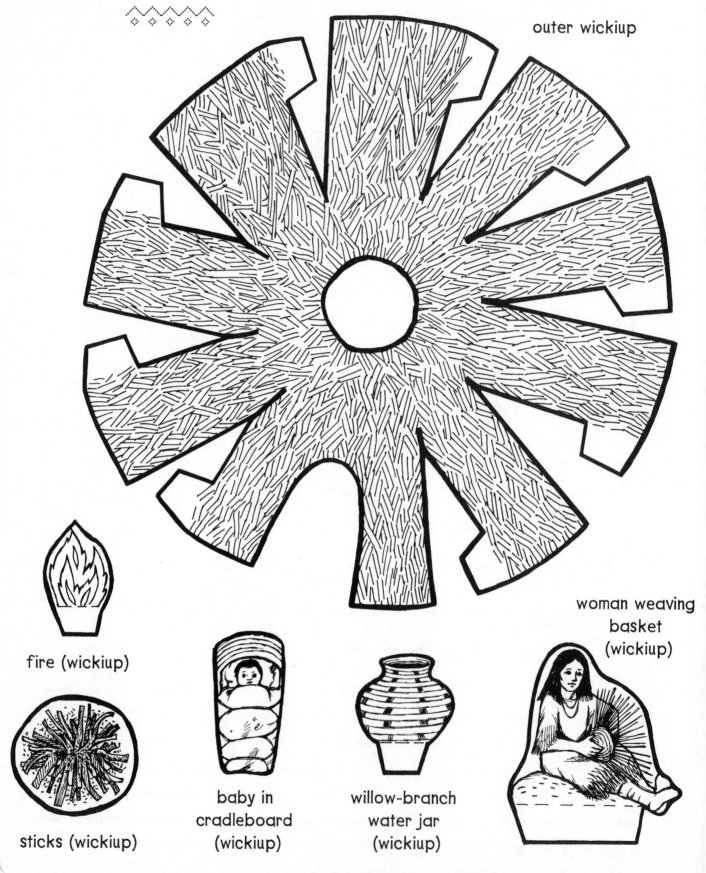

outer wickiup

fire (wickiup)

sticks (wickiup)

baby in cradleboard (wickiup)

willow-branch water jar (wickiup)

woman weaving basket (wickiup)

Easy Make & Learn Projects: Southwest Indians   Scholastic Teaching Resources

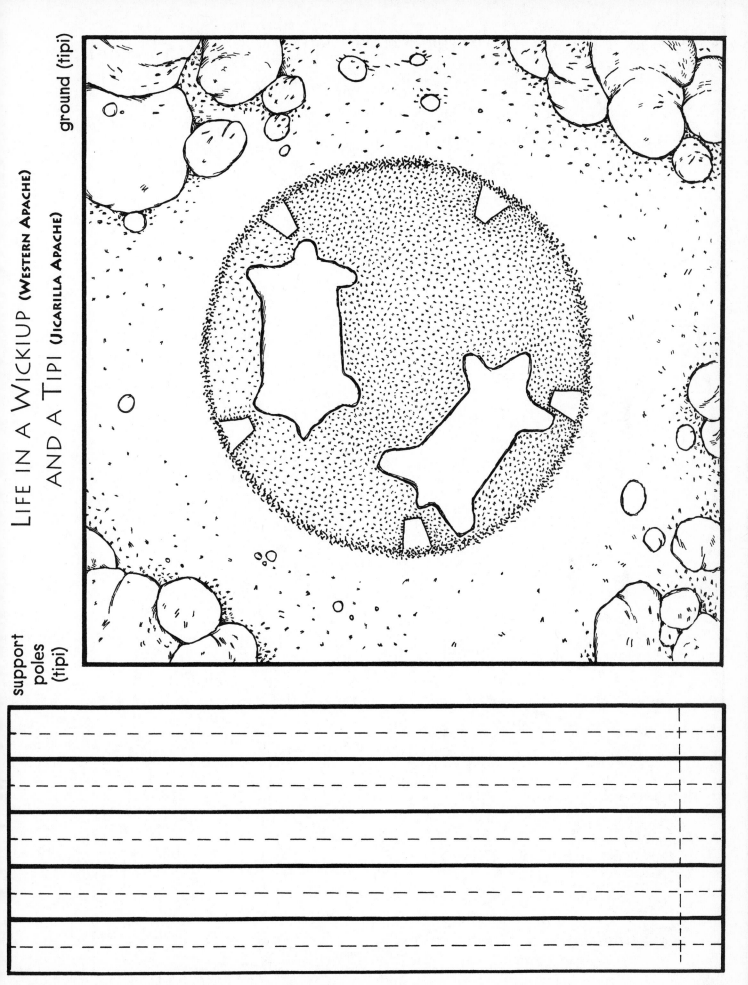

LIFE IN A WICKIUP (WESTERN APACHE) AND A TIPI (JICARILLA APACHE)

ground (tipi)

support poles (tipi)

LIFE IN A WICKIUP (WESTERN APACHE)
AND A TIPI (JICARILLA APACHE)

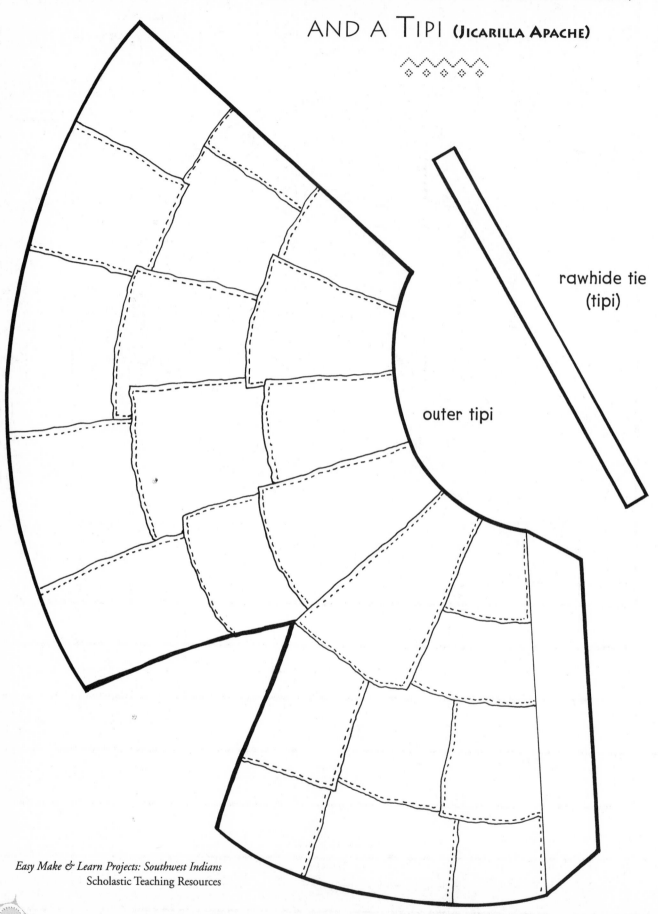

rawhide tie
(tipi)

outer tipi

LIFE IN A WICKIUP (WESTERN APACHE) AND A TIPI (JICARILLA APACHE)

people
(tipi)

fire
(tipi)

sticks
(tipi)

baskets
(tipi)

saddlebags
(tipi)

dog
(tipi)

Easy Make & Learn Projects: Southwest Indians
Scholastic Teaching Resources

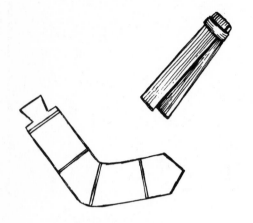

Cactus Fruit Tongs

Hunter's Throwing Stick

Finding Food Diorama

(HOPI, ZUNI)

Students make models of tools
used by the Hopi and Zuni tribes
to obtain foods.

NATIVE TRADITIONS

I n addition to raising crops, Hopi Indians hunted animals and gathered fruits to feed their families. The men used arrows shot from bows to kill large prey, such as deer. They used carved, curved throwing sticks of wood (similar to boomerangs), about three feet wide, to hit rabbits and other small game. The curved end helped the stick gain momentum as it spun through the air.

Among the plants that the Hopi gathered to eat were nuts, seeds, berries, and the bright red fruits of the prickly pear cactus. To gather the fruit without being stuck by the cacti's sharp spines, Hopi women used tongs made out of the stiff fibers of a dead cactus. Since the outer covering of the cactus fruit is also covered with sharp spines, they put the gathered fruit in flat baskets and used a stone to rub off the prickly spines or burned them off. The Hopi not only ate the bright red fruit, they also made dye from it.

MAKING THE MODELS

Guide students in following these directions to make their models:

✠ Cactus Fruit Tongs and Hunter's Throwing Stick ✠

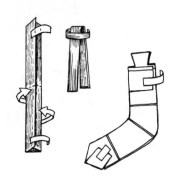

1 Cut out the patterns on page 40. Fold the TONGS in thirds lengthwise to form one long rectangle, and tape closed.

2 Fold the TONGS in half the short way. Then wrap the TONG TIE around the folded end of the TONGS and tape.

3 Fold the THROWING STICK along the dotted line, fold down the flaps, and tape closed.

✠ Finding Food Diorama ✠

1 Fold the two-sided scene on page 41 in half along the dotted line. Then tape closed near the bottom of each side.

2 Tape the ends of the FRUIT-PICKING STRIP to each side of its corresponding scene. Repeat with the HUNTING STRIP on the other side of the diorama. The STRIPS will curve as shown.

3 Rest the THROWING STICK and TONGS on the STRIPS in front of the appropriate scene.

TEACHING WITH THE MODELS

1 How did the Hopi obtain food? (*They farmed, gathered, and hunted.*)

2 What kinds of animals did Hopi men hunt? (*They hunted large animals such as deer and smaller game such as rabbits.*)

3 What kinds of food did the Hopi gather? (*They gathered nuts, seeds, berries, and fruit from cacti.*)

4 How did the Hopi protect themselves when picking and preparing cactus fruit? (*They used tongs to protect themselves from sharp cactus spines. They rubbed off the spines on the fruit with stones or burned them off.*)

Materials

- photocopies of pages 40–41 for each student
- scissors
- tape
- crayons, colored pencils, or markers (optional)

Do More!

The Hopi and Zuni gathered the fruit of the prickly pear cactus for food and for making plant dye. These tribes, as well as others in the Southwest, also gathered plant parts (such as leaves, roots, stems or stalks, nuts, and flowers) for a variety of uses. Challenge students to research and report on some of these plants and the ways in which different parts were used.

Cactus Fruit Tongs
Hunter's Throwing Stick

(Hopi, Zuni)

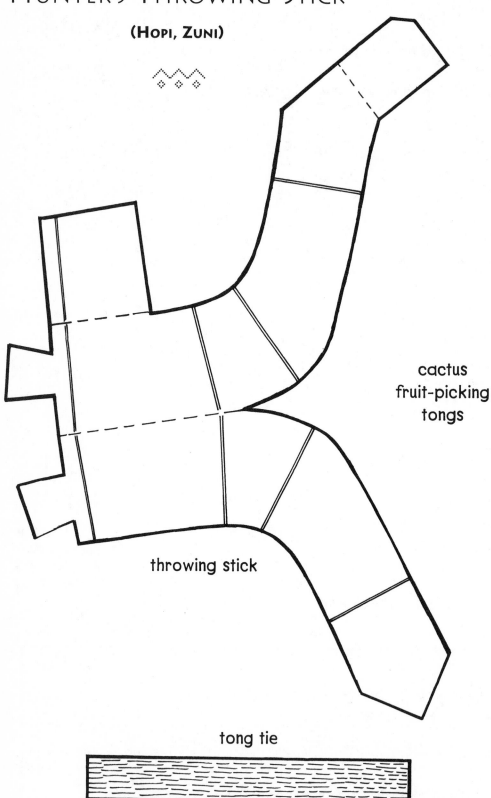

cactus
fruit-picking
tongs

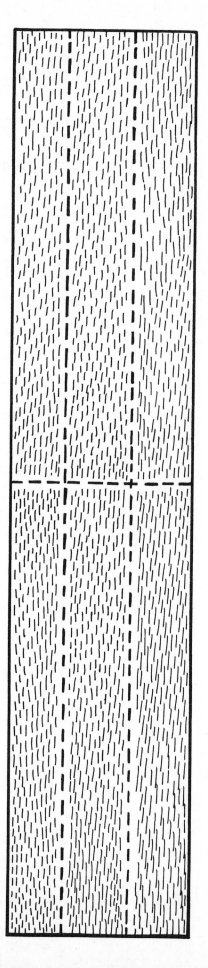

throwing stick

tong tie

Easy Make & Learn Projects: Southwest Indians   Scholastic Teaching Resources

FINDING FOOD DIORAMA

(HOPI, ZUNI)

hunting scene

fruit-picking scene

hunting strip

Hunting rabbits with a throwing stick.

Picking prickly pear cactus fruit with tongs.

fruit-picking strip

Growing Corn Fold-Up Book

(ZUNI)

Cooking With Corn Storyboard

(HOPI)

Students make a mini-book and a storyboard to learn about the importance of corn in Southwest Indian cultures.

NATIVE TRADITIONS

Corn was the major crop raised by the Zuni and the Hopi. The Zuni built waffle-shaped squares with walls in the ground in which to plant corn. Then they used sticks to dig the holes for planting the seeds. Farmers filled each square with water to enable the corn kernels to sprout into tiny plants. They tended the crop until the corn was ripe for harvesting.

One of the dishes that Hopi women made from corn was a paper-thin flat bread called *piki* (PEE-kee). Using a handstone that looked like a rolling pin, they ground dried blue corn into fine meal on a stone block. Then they mixed it with water to prepare a thin batter that they spread with their bare hand over a greased, heated stone called a *duma*. Baking piki required an especially skillful cook who could spread the batter fast enough to avoid burning her hand. The piki baked quickly and could be peeled easily off the stone and rolled into a cylinder.

The women also baked cornbread in beehive-shaped ovens and used flat wooden paddles to remove them when they were done. (It is not clear whether the Spanish introduced this kind of oven, but before their arrival, the Hopi used ovens of different kinds.)

Hopi women made another dish by filling two cornhusks with sweet corn mush. Then they rolled the filled husks and tied them closed with a strand of husk before steaming them. The Spanish later named these *tamales*.

MAKING THE MODELS

Guide students in following these directions to make their models:

1 Color pages 44–46 as desired. Cut apart the pages of the fold-up book on page 44 for use in Teaching With the Model, below.

2 On page 45, use the point of a scissors to cut open the six slits along the thick black lines.

3 Cut out the five pieces on page 46. Fit the three WOMEN and the CORN FILLING into the corresponding slits on page 45, and secure with tape on the back. Then tape the ROLLED AND FILLED CORN HUSKS to the appropriate place on the storyboard.

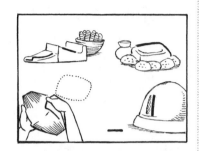

TEACHING WITH THE MODELS

1 Ask students to study the mini-book pages and use the text and pictures to put the pages in order. Then have them number the pages and tape them together, side by side to make an accordion book. If students would like to mount the pages onto construction paper, have them accordion fold the construction paper strip into six equal sections. Then they can tape each page, in order, onto the panels.

2 Encourage students to explain in their own words how the Zuni grew corn.

3 Ask students to use their models to describe the different tools used by the Hopi for preparing and cooking corn dishes. (*grinding stone, handstone that resembled a rolling pin, heated stones, jugs for holding water, clay pots for holding ears of corn and batter, stone griddle, beehive-shaped oven*) What are some of the corn dishes they made? (*flat bread called* piki, *corn husks filled with sweet corn mush*)

Materials

- photocopies of pages 44–46 for each student
- scissors
- tape

OPTIONAL:

- 4- by 24-inch sheets of construction paper
- glue sticks
- crayons, colored pencils, or markers

Do More!

Invite students to read a firsthand description of how piki bread is made at Acacia Artisans Stories & Facts (www.acaciart.com/stories/piki.html). Then follow up with a fascinating streaming video of a Hopi woman making traditional piki bread at Viewseum (www.viewseum.com/viewseum/spotlight/native_americans/Lifestyle/frybread.htm).

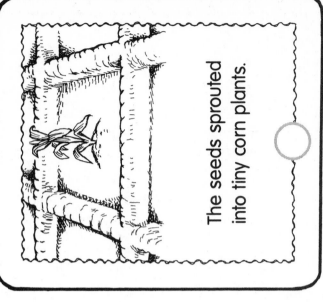

The Zuni created
a waffle-shaped
area in the ground.

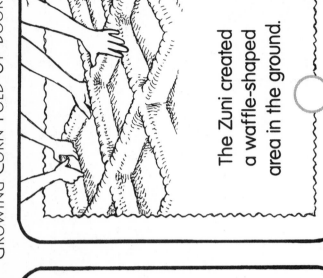

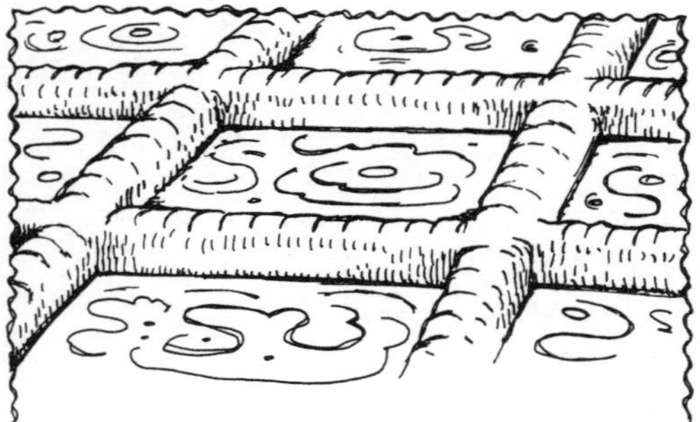

The seeds sprouted
into tiny corn plants.

Scholastic Teaching Resources

Growing Corn

�֍
֍   ֍

When the corn was ripe,
the Zuni harvested
the crop.

Easy Make & Learn Projects: Southwest Indians

Using sticks, they poked
a hole in each square
and planted a corn kernel.

They filled each square
with water.

Cooking with Corn Storyboard (Hopi)

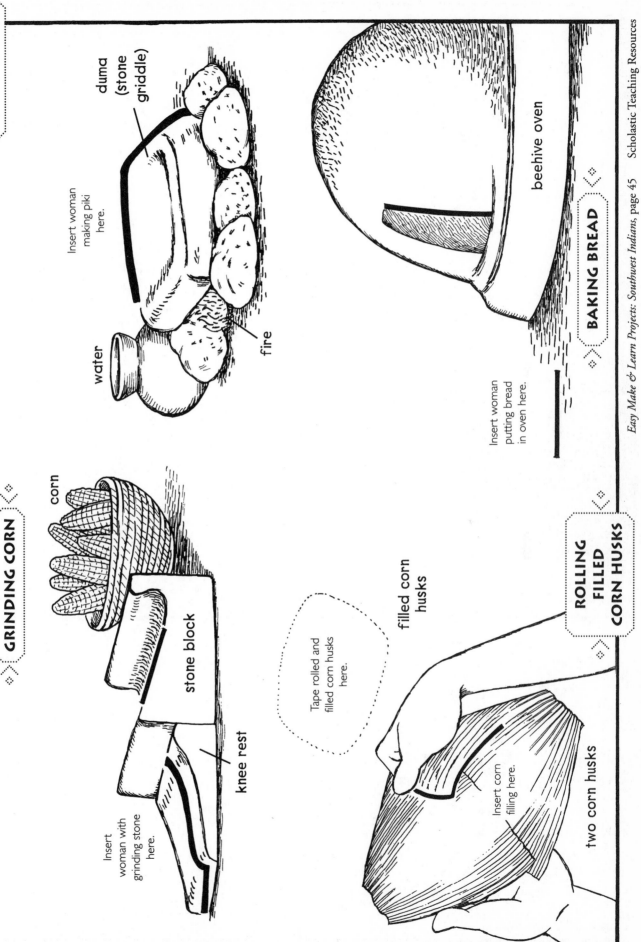

duma (stone griddle)

Insert woman making piki here.

water

fire

BAKING BREAD

beehive oven

Insert woman putting bread in oven here.

GRINDING CORN

corn

stone block

knee rest

Insert woman with grinding stone here.

Tape rolled and filled corn husks here.

filled corn husks

ROLLING FILLED CORN HUSKS

Insert corn filling here.

two corn husks

Cooking with Corn Storyboard (Hopi)

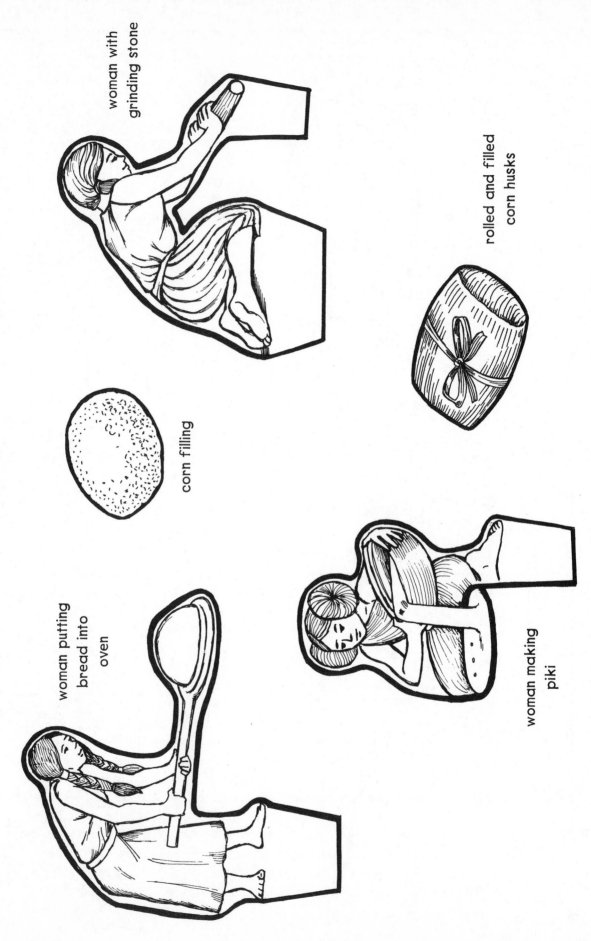

woman with grinding stone

corn filling

rolled and filled corn husks

woman putting bread into oven

woman making piki

Easy Make & Learn Projects: Southwest Indians   Scholastic Teaching Resources

On the Move

A Roasted Desert Dish

(MESCALERO APACHE)

Students make a model that demonstrates
the importance of horses to the Apache,
and one that shows how they roasted a desert plant.

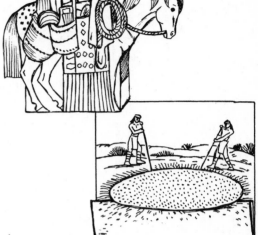

NATIVE TRADITIONS

Like other Apache tribes, the Mescalero were often on the move. Whether they were in the mountains, the desert, or hunting buffalo on the Great Plains, the Mescalero relied on horses to transport them and their belongings. Burden baskets, blankets, bows and arrows, moccasins and clothing, water containers, and shelter were carefully packed and secured on the strong backs of horses. (Point out to students that although horses were introduced into the Southwest by Spanish explorers who started arriving around 1540, tribes such as the Apache adopted and bred horses that had escaped from the Spanish into the wild from regions farther south prior to that time.)

As they moved, the Mescalero took advantage of the plants and animals they found. They gathered grasses, fruits, flowers, pods, berries, roots, nuts, seeds, and bark. They hunted sheep, deer, rabbits, birds, and other game.

One of the most important foods for the Mescalero was from the *agave* or century plant. The Mescalero cut the leaves and the stalks of the agave plant and roasted them in a pit that was usually about twelve feet across and four feet deep. In the pit, they made a fire among rocks. On top of the fire, they placed the chopped parts of the agave plants and covered them with wet grasses and then with about three feet of earth. The agave baked for three to five days. The Mescalero dried any excess roasted agave in the sun to store it. Later they prepared the vegetable for eating by soaking it in water to soften it. Roasted agave is a sweet, juicy, and stringy vegetable that tastes like a cross between squash and sweet potatoes.

Materials

- photocopies of pages 50–52 for each student
- scissors
- tape
- crayons, colored pencils, or markers (optional)

MAKING THE MODELS

On the Move

Guide students in following these directions to make their model:

1 Color pages 50–52 as desired. Then cut out the HORSE on page 50 and fold up each side along the dotted lines.

2 Fold the four tabs at the front and back of the HORSE and tape. Also, tape along the head and back of the horse as shown.

3 Cut out the SADDLEBAGS on page 51 and the curved slits on them. Fold the pattern in half lengthwise along the long dotted line, and tape closed as shown. Then fold the SADDLEBAGS in half along the short dotted line.

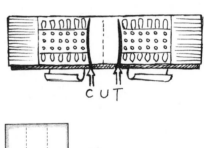
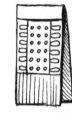

4 Cut out the BLANKETS on pages 51–52. Fold each lengthwise, into thirds, and tape closed. Then fold the BLANKETS in half along the short dotted line.

5 Cut out the BURDEN BASKETS on page 51. Fold along the dotted line.

6 Cut out the TWINED-BASKET WATER JAR/BURDEN BASKET on page 52. Cut open the slit, fold back the flap, and tape as shown. Then fold along the dotted line.

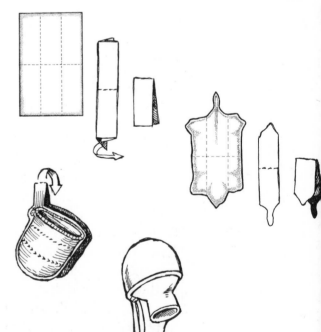

7 Set aside these items and then cut out the remaining items on pages 51–52 for use in Teaching With the Model, page 49.

✂ *A Roasted Desert Dish* ✂

Guide students in following these directions to make their model:

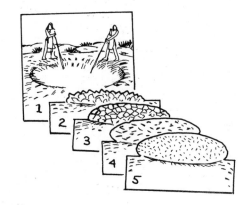

1 Color page 53 as desired. Then cut out the patterns.

2 Stack the patterns 2–5 in order so that 2 is on the bottom and 5 is on the top.

3 Align the stack with the bottom of the BACKGROUND and staple twice as shown.

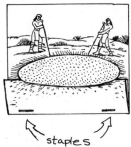

staples

TEACHING WITH THE MODELS

1 Where did the Mescalero Apache travel? (*They traveled in the mountains and the deserts of the Southwest and in the Great Plains.*)

2 Invite students to choose items to pack on their horse. Have them think about the function of each item as they make their choices. Then ask them to use their models to identify the items their horses are transporting and explain why they chose these items to pack. (*Answers will vary.*)

3 What did the Mescalero gather and hunt? (*They gathered grasses, fruits, and so on, and hunted sheep, deer, and other game.*)

4 What is agave, and how did the Mescalero use it? (*Agave is a desert plant that was a staple of the Mescalero's diet. The Mescalero roasted it in deep pits.*)

5 Starting with the bottom layer, encourage students to lift each layer on their Desert Dish models to read about how the Mescalero prepared the agave for roasting.

Do More!

Agave is just one kind of plant that grows in the Chihuahuan and Sonoran deserts in the southwestern United States. Challenge students to research other plants that grow in these deserts and create a desert plant field guide. For each page of the field guide, students can draw a picture of a plant and write about its size, life cycle, characteristics that make it adapted to desert conditions, and so on.

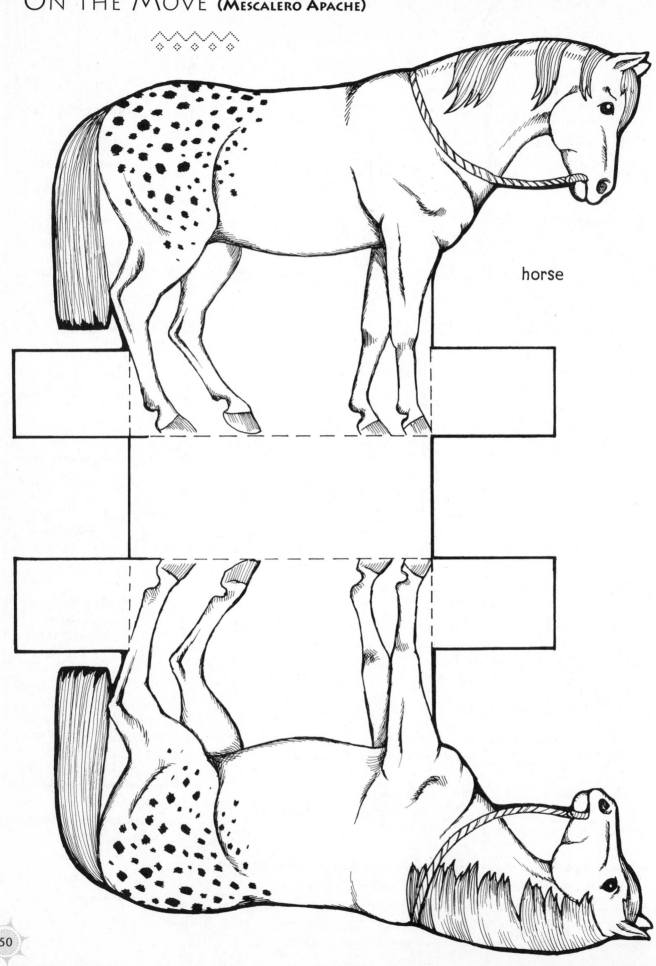

horse

ON THE MOVE
(MESCALERO APACHE)

rope-twisting tool

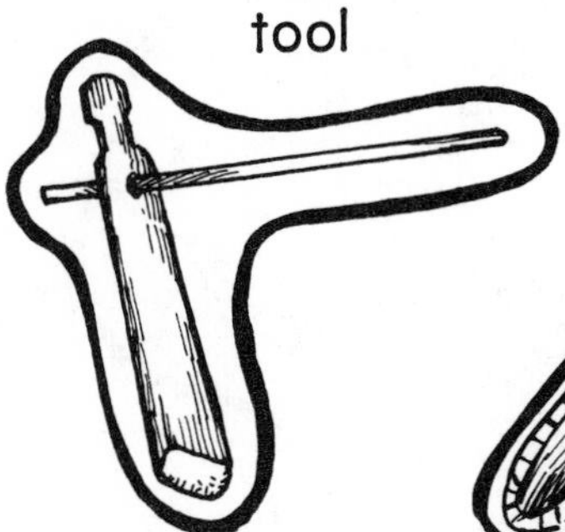

burden baskets

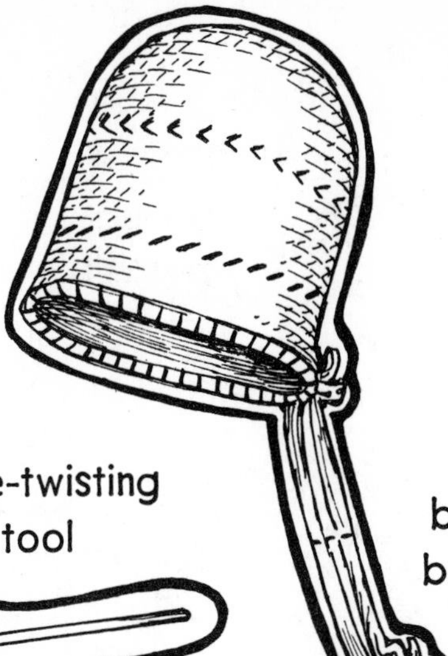

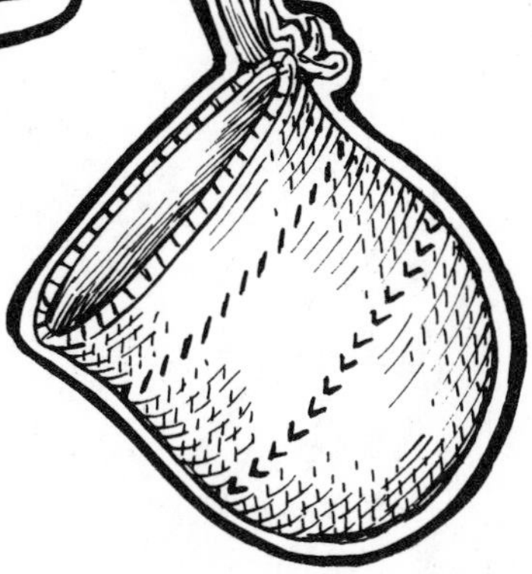

blanket

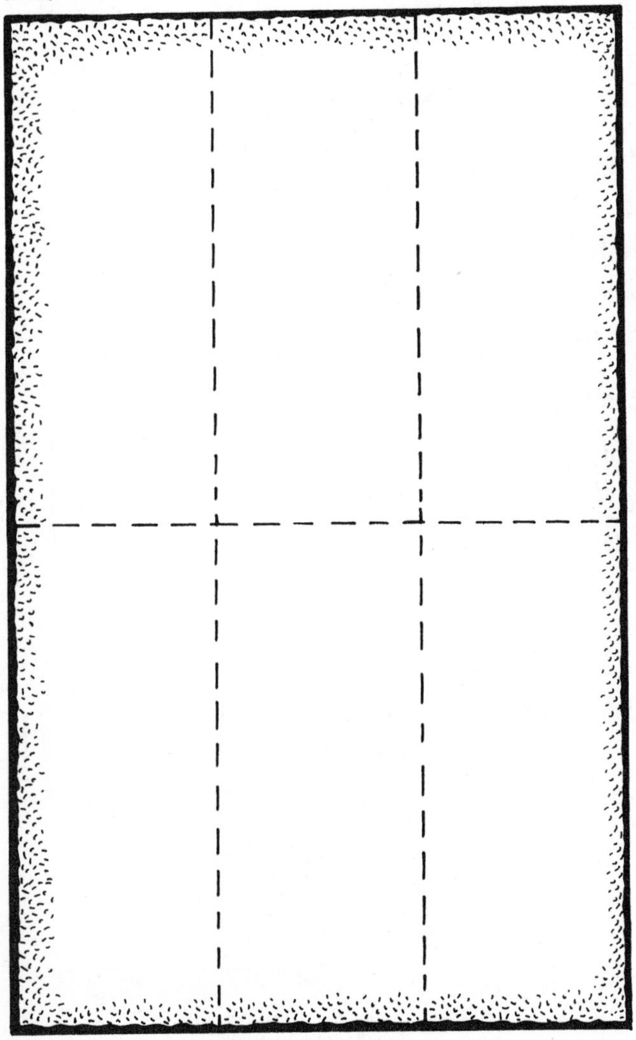

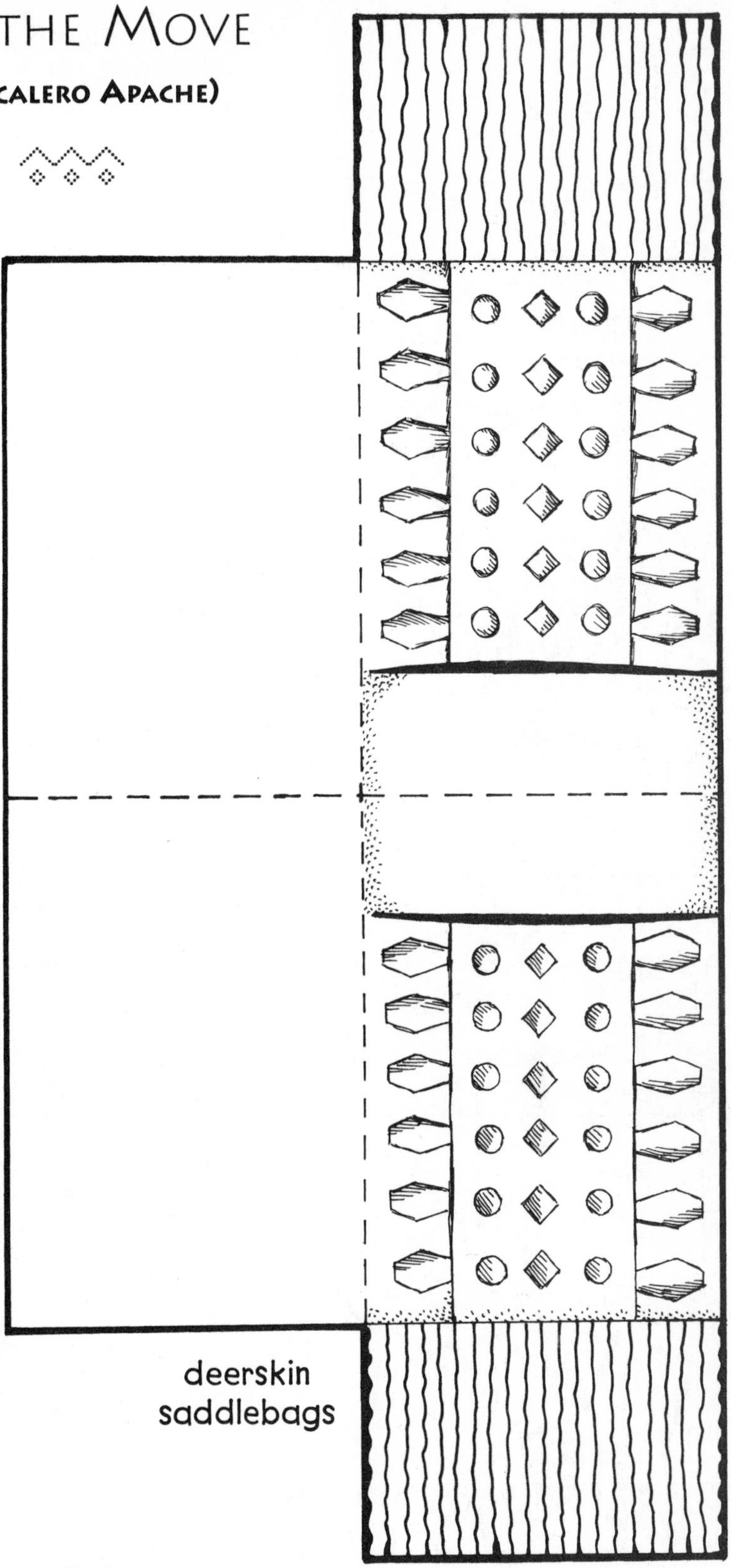

deerskin saddlebags

arrow-straightening tool

hole-punching tool

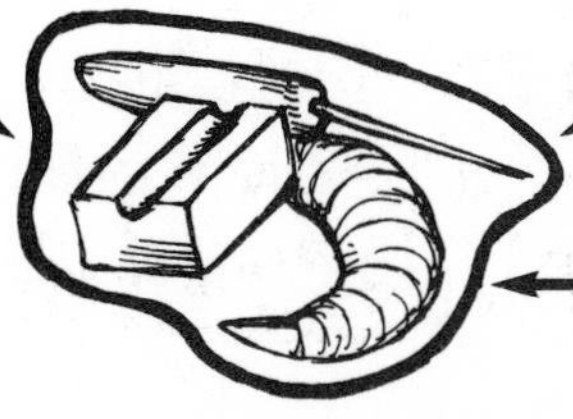

hide-scraping tool

ON THE MOVE (MESCALERO APACHE)

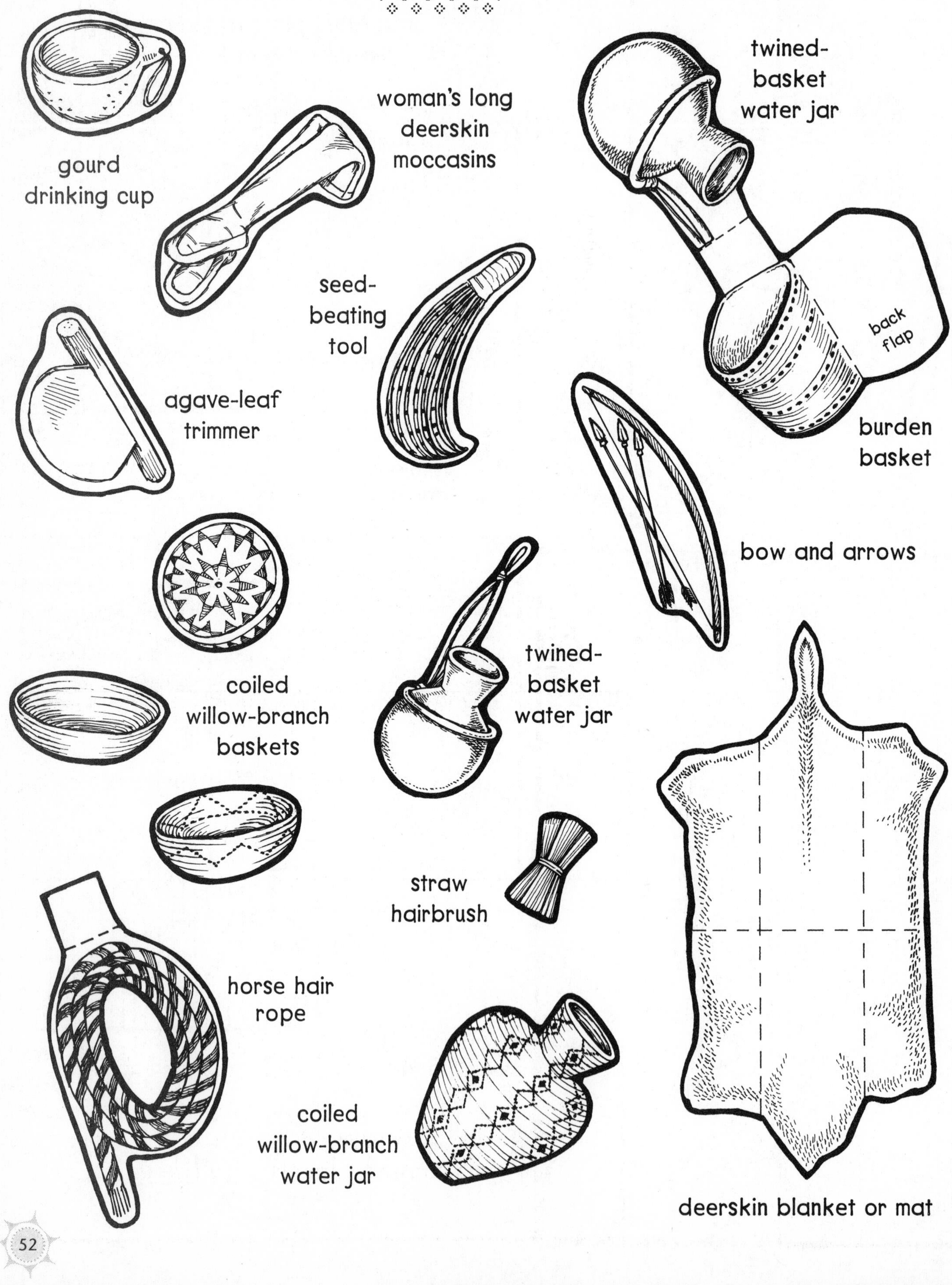

gourd
drinking cup

woman's long
deerskin
moccasins

twined-
basket
water jar

seed-
beating
tool

agave-leaf
trimmer

back
flap

burden
basket

bow and arrows

coiled
willow-branch
baskets

twined-
basket
water jar

horse hair
rope

straw
hairbrush

coiled
willow-branch
water jar

deerskin blanket or mat

Easy Make & Learn Projects: Southwest Indians   Scholastic Teaching Resources

Easy Make & Learn Projects: Southwest Indians, page 53 Scholastic Teaching Resources

ROASTING AGAVE

Agave was an important plant to the Mescalero Apache.

2 Then they built a fire among rocks.

1 First the Mescalero dug a big pit (sometimes 20 feet across).

A ROASTED DESERT DISH
(MESCALERO APACHE)

4 Then they covered it with wet grass.

3 Next they put chopped agave in the pit.

5 Last, they covered the agave with earth and roasted it for three to five days.

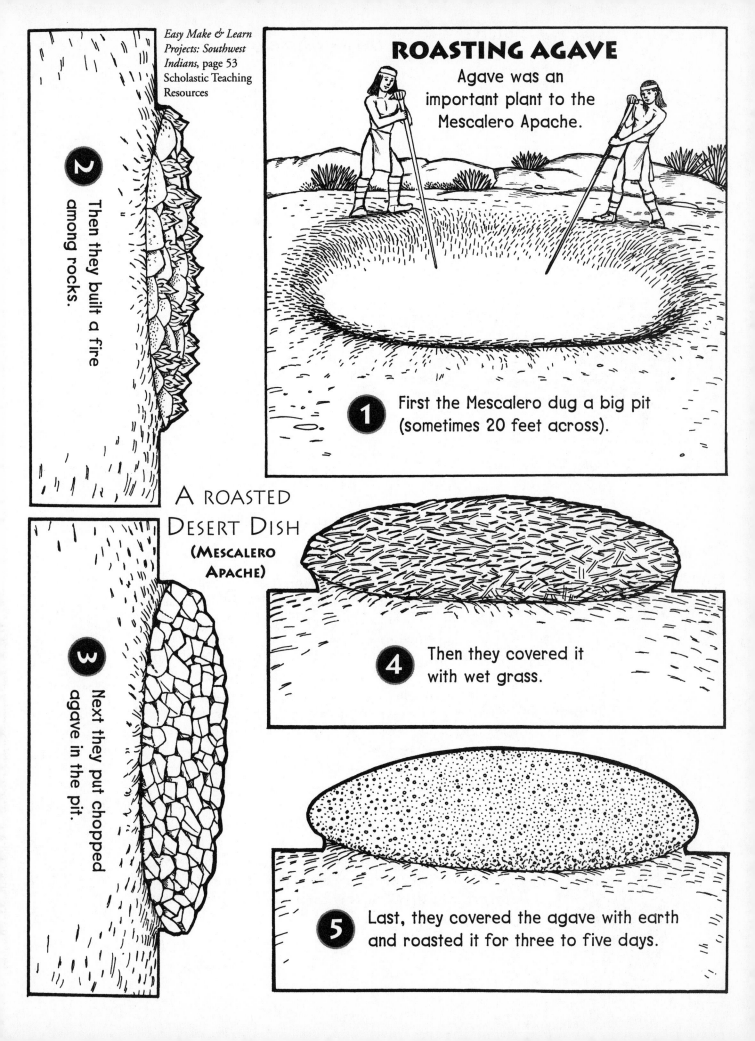

How Deer Were Used Diorama

(APACHE)

Students make a diorama
to learn how the Apache
depended on deer.

NATIVE TRADITIONS

Several kinds of deer roamed the Southwest, and the Apache hunted them along with elk, mountain sheep, and other game. Like the Indians of the Great Plains who used almost every part of a buffalo, the Apache used deer in many ways.

They ate deer meat and used other parts of the animal including bones, blood, sinew, and hide. To prepare a deer hide for use, the Apache scraped it with tools made from deer bones and soaked the hide in water for a few days. Then the wet hide was laid over a pole, and the hair was removed with a horse rib. The hide was left in the sun for a few days and pounded with a stone to thin it into rawhide. To turn rawhide into soft buckskin, the Apache worked warm water and boiled deer brains into it. Then they hung the hide in the sun and stretched it.

The Apache used hides, rawhide, and buckskin for moccasins, wrist guards, robes, containers, blankets, and as coverings for their dwellings. They sewed with deer sinew, which they also used for bowstrings and to attach feathers to arrows. They mixed deer blood with plant poisons and rubbed the mixture on arrowheads to make the points deadlier.

Before embarking on a deer hunt, Apache men often fasted and took part in ceremonies. Sometimes they wore deer-head masks and clothing that was the color of deer when they stalked their prey. When a hunter made a kill, he shared it with the other men in the hunting party.

MAKING THE MODEL

Guide students in following these directions to make their models:

1 Color pages 56–57 as desired. Then cut out the BACKGROUND, BASE, and FOREGROUND.

2 Fold up the tabs on the BASE along the dotted lines.

3 Curve the BACKGROUND around the BASE so that the fold-up tabs are behind the BACKGROUND. Tape the tabs to the back of the BACKGROUND as shown.

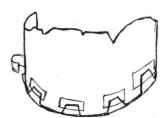

4 Fold in the tabs on the FOREGROUND. Then tape them to each side of the BACKGROUND as shown.

5 Cut out the remaining pieces and place inside or outside the diorama as desired.

TEACHING WITH THE MODEL

1 What animals did the Apache hunt? (*deer, elk, mountain sheep, and other wild game*)

2 How did the Apache use deer? (*They ate deer meat for food, used the bones as tools, and turned hides into rawhide and buckskin. They used hides, rawhide, and buckskin for moccasins, wrist guards, robes, containers, blankets, and coverings for their homes.*)

3 Ask students to study their diorama and read about the different uses of deer. Encourage them to look up words they might not know, such as *quiver* or *sinew*.

4 Why did the Indians wear deer-head masks and clothing similar in color to deerskin when they stalked deer? (*Possible answer: They hoped to fool or confuse the deer and get close without scaring them away.*)

Materials

- photocopies of pages 56–57
- scissors
- tape
- crayons, colored pencils, or markers (optional)

Do More!

Wearing deer-head masks and deer-colored clothing helped Apache hunters approach their prey without being detected. Explain to students that in nature, animal predators rely on camouflage and other adaptations to creep up on their prey without being seen. Many prey also rely on being able to blend into the plants and rocks around them to escape capture. Let students research and report on the different forms of camouflage animals use to help them stay alive.

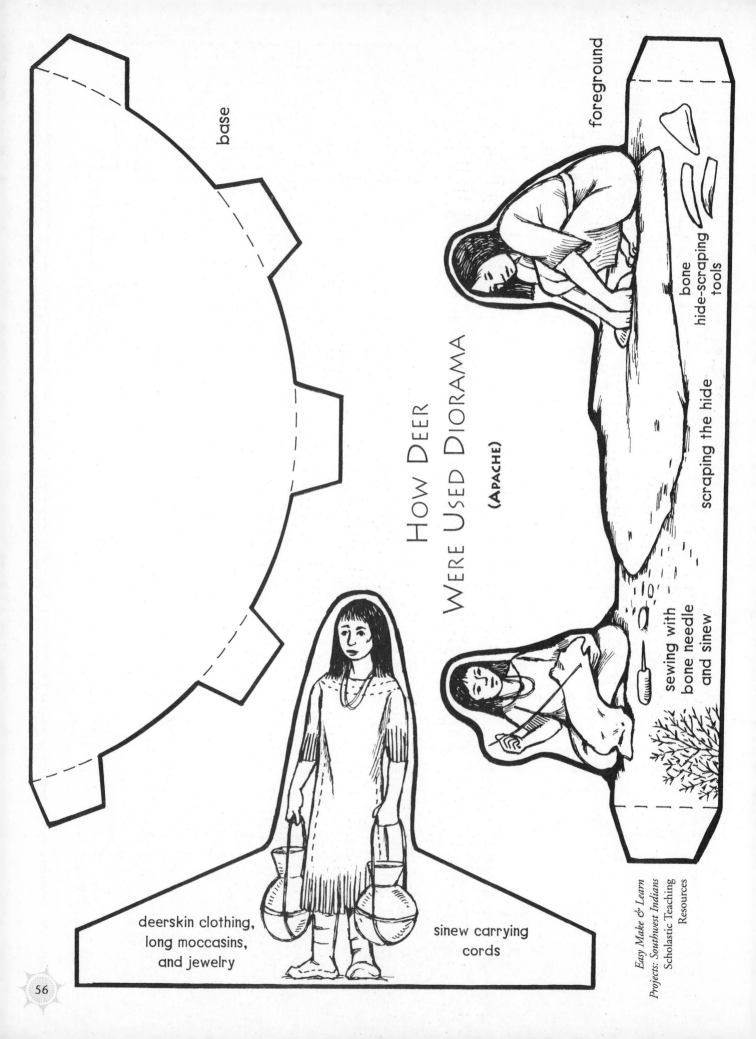

base

foreground

bone
hide-scraping
tools

scraping the hide

sewing with
bone needle
and sinew

How Deer
Were Used Diorama
(Apache)

deerskin clothing,
long moccasins,
and jewelry

sinew carrying
cords

*Easy Make & Learn
Projects: Southwest Indians*
Scholastic Teaching
Resources

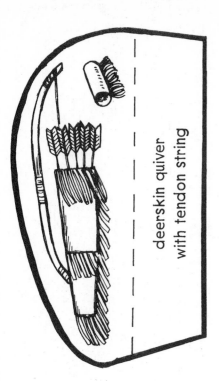

deerskin quiver
with tendon string

How Deer Were Used Diorama

(Apache)

buckskin
cradleboard
cover

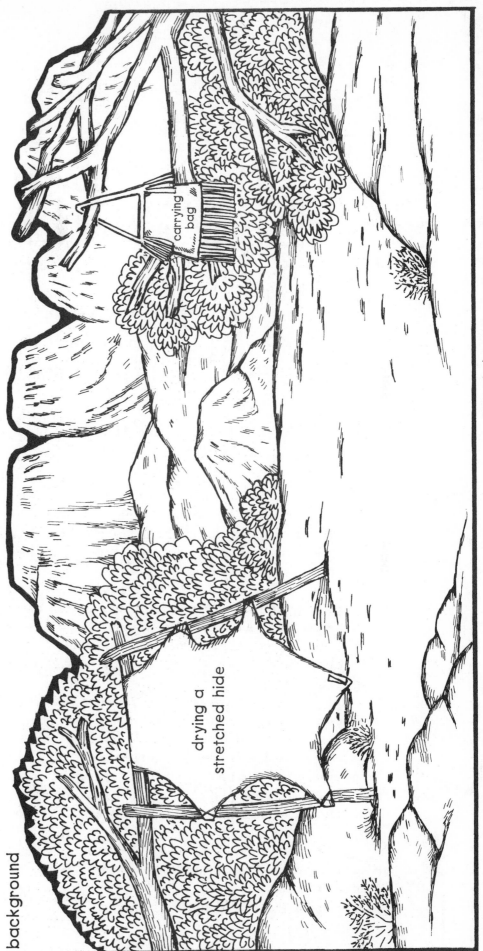

carrying bag

drying a stretched hide

background

Painted Pottery

How to Make a Zuni Pot Mini-Book

(ZUNI)

Students make a model of Zuni pottery and a mini-book that describes how pots were made.

NATIVE TRADITIONS

For thousands of years, Native Americans in the Southwest have been producing pottery that is both beautiful and useful. Today, these bowls, storage jars, and other ceramic works are highly valued works of art among Indians and non-Indians alike.

Every pueblo had quarries, and each potter had a section from which to dig clay. The potter dried the clay and then cleaned it by passing it through a sieve. Then the clay was prepared with earth or mica, and water was added to make it workable.

To form the pots, a potter first created a base and then layered long, thin coils of clay one on top of another and pinched them together. Then she used her fingers and a paddle made of broken pottery to join the base to the clay coils and to shape the pot and thin the sides. After the pot had partially dried, the potter used an abrasive stone, such as pumice, to sand and smooth it. A paint-like mixture of white clay and water called *slip* was then applied and the pot was polished using a piece of flint. To decorate the pot, the potter painted designs using black paint and a brush made from the fibers of a yucca plant. She then added colors and polished the pot again. The pot sat for a few days to dry before it was fired in a mound-like kiln fueled by dried animal dung. The heat from the fire would change the color, so that a pot painted yellow-ocher would turn red.

Women created the pottery used in ceremonies by decorating the pieces with symbols for water, clouds, the sun, and animals along with curved lines and other motifs. Water pots, called *ollas*, were shaped so a woman could balance the full pot on her head as she walked home from a spring.

MAKING THE MODELS

Guide students in following these directions to make their models:

1 Color page 60 as desired. Cut out the mini-book page along the outer solid lines. Fold the page in half widthwise, and then in half again to make the mini-book.

2 Choose one of the POTS on page 61 or 62 and cut it out.

3 Glue or tape the blank POT in the center of the colored paper.

4 Study the DESIGNS on pages 61–63. Cut out the DESIGNS you would like to use to decorate your POT. Glue or tape them in place. Color as desired. You can also draw your own designs.

TEACHING WITH THE MODELS

1 Where did the Zuni find clay for their pottery? (*Each village had quarries, and each potter had her special section to dig.*)

2 How did the Zuni create their pottery? (*They dug the clay, cleaned and prepared it, and shaped it into a pot. Then they smoothed, sanded, applied paint-like clay, decorated, polished, and fired it.*)

3 What are *ollas*, and what is special about their shape? (Ollas *are water pots with special shapes that allowed women to carry them on their heads.*)

4 Ask students to display their pottery designs and explain what they think their designs symbolize. Have them compare their designs to the Zuni pot on the cover of their mini-books. (*Answers will vary.*)

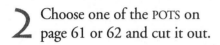

Materials

* photocopies of pages 60–63 for each student
* scissors
* glue sticks or tape
* construction or colored paper
* crayons, colored pencils, or markers (optional)

Do More!

Visit the Clayhound Web Site: Native American Traditional Pottery (www.clayhound.us/sites/anasazi.htm) to see examples of traditional Pueblo pottery from as early as 500. The site features photographs from each of the 21 Pueblos as well as from other southwestern tribes.

After students study the pottery, provide them with clay. Invite them to make clay ropes, and then coil and pinch them together to shape and form a pot, bowl, or cup. Students can decorate their objects by using toothpicks to draw symbols or by fashioning symbols from clay and pressing them on the object.

2

Once the pot had dried a little, the potter smoothed it using a rough stone. Then she applied a paint-like mixture of white clay, called *slip*.

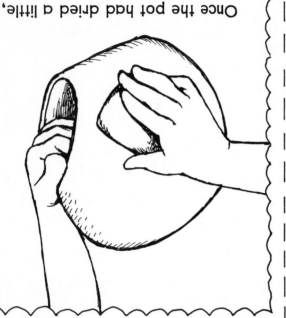

1

First the potter layered long coils of clay, pinched them together, and thinned them using her fingers and a paddle of broken pottery.

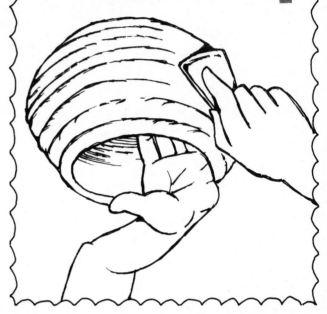

3

To paint designs on the pot, she used a yucca plant fiber brush. Then, after polishing, she fired the pot in a mound-like oven fueled by dried animal waste, called *dung*.

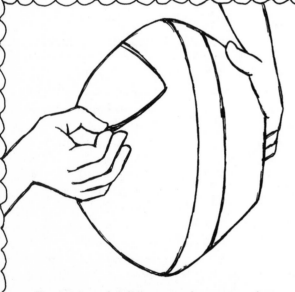

HOW TO MAKE A ZUNI POT

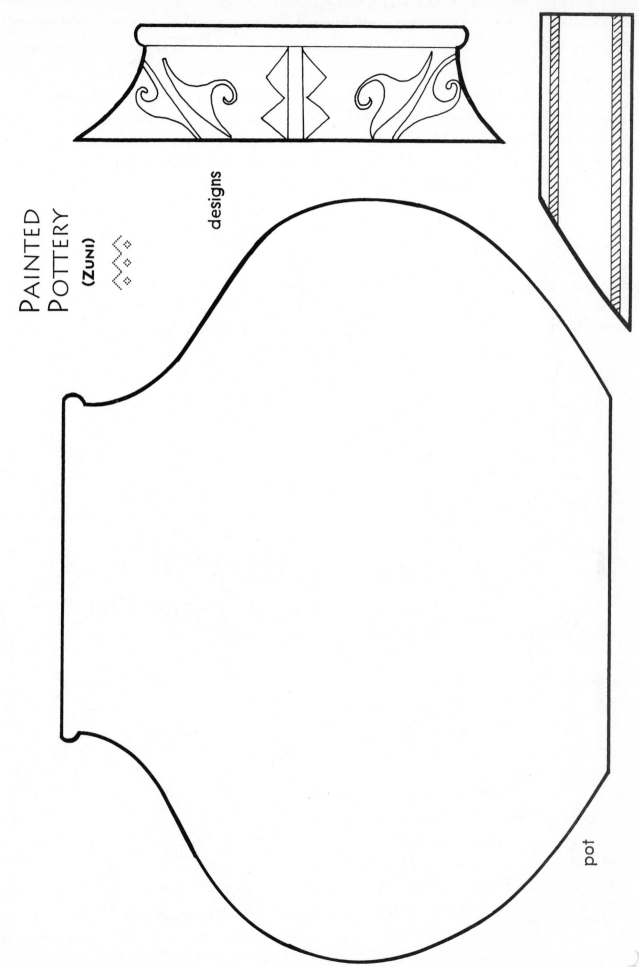

PAINTED POTTERY

(ZUNI)

designs

pot

PAINTED POTTERY
(ZUNI)

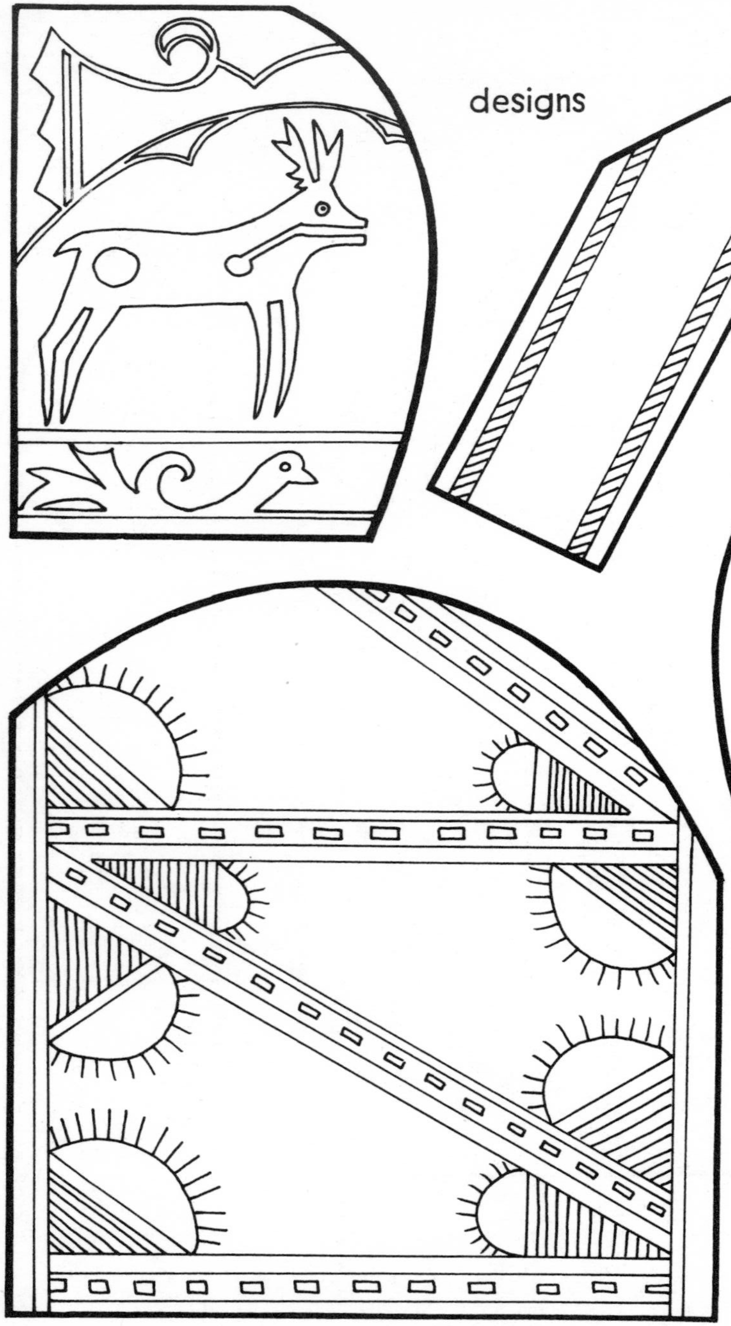

pot

designs

Easy Make & Learn Projects: Southwest Indians   Scholastic Teaching Resources

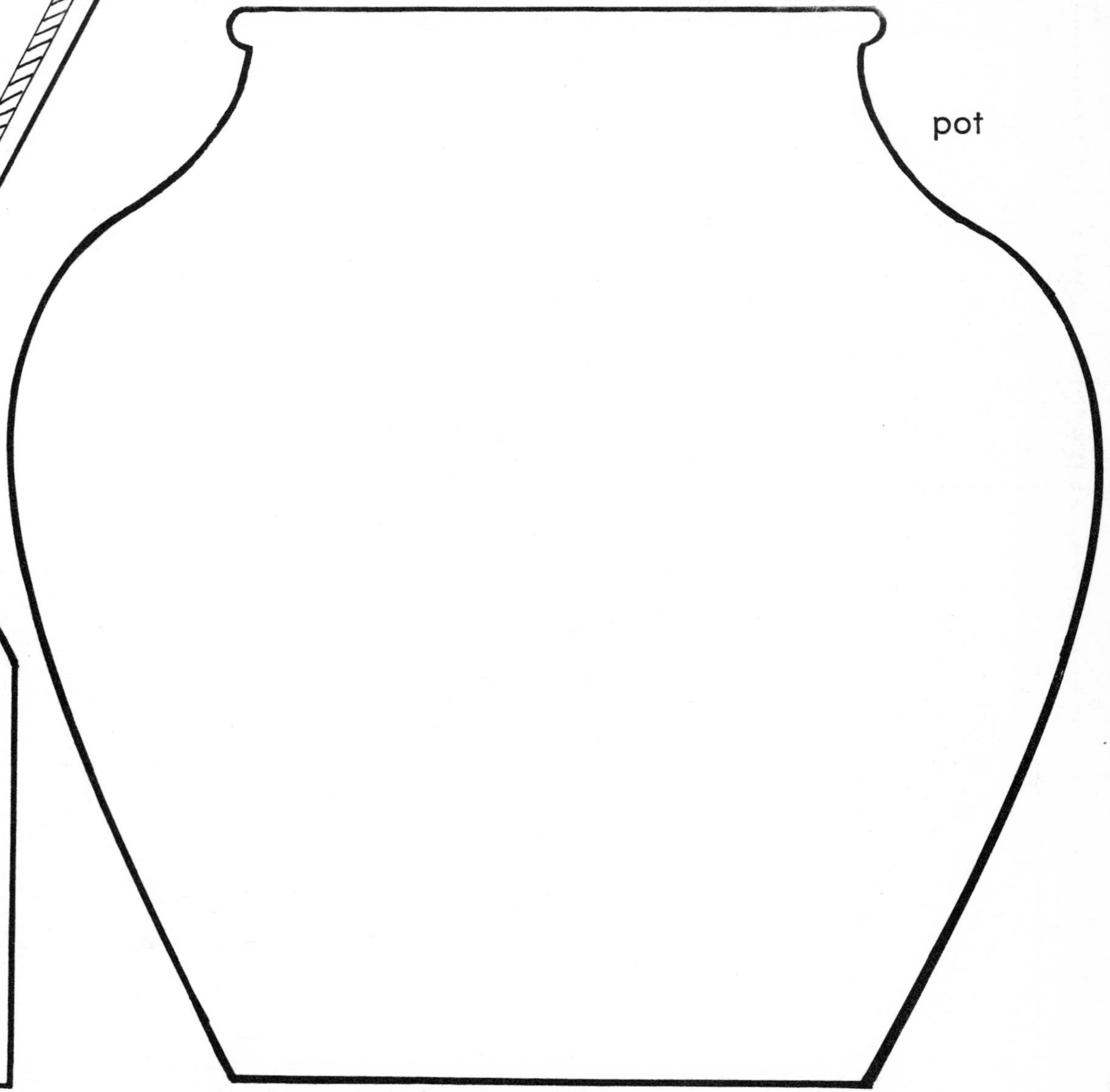

designs

PAINTED POTTERY
(ZUNI)

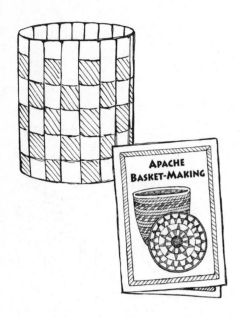

Weave a Basket

(WESTERN APACHE AND JICARILLA APACHE)

Apache Basket-Making Mini-Book

Students weave a model of a basket and make a mini-book that describes Apache basket-making.

NATIVE TRADITIONS

The Apache tribes didn't make many pottery containers like the pueblo-dwelling Indians did. Instead, they depended on sturdy woven baskets (burden baskets) to carry things from place to place on horseback. (See On the Move, page 47, for more.) They also wove baskets to carry and store corn and other foods. In addition, they used baskets to hold water, as trays, and in ceremonies.

In the Apache tribes, women were the basket makers. To make baskets, they began by gathering reeds, willow or cottonwood branches, and other raw materials, and scraping and stripping—and sometimes splitting—them. The material was then placed in water or buried in hot sand to make it softer and more pliable.

The basket weaver had to decide the size and shape of a basket as well as how to decorate it. This took great concentration and skill. For instance, to create a water container, a weaver had to prepare pitch—a resin produced from the sap inside piñon trees—to seal the container and prevent leaks. To make a basket or tray, a weaver would bundle flexible willow boughs together and then coil and sew them into a basket.

Weavers also wove twined baskets by alternately passing specially prepared flexible branches or strips over and under each other to form a checkered or other type of pattern. Apache women often decorated their work with geometric patterns, and later, with pictures of animals and people. The Western Apache and the Jicarilla Apache especially became known for their basket-making skills.

MAKING THE MODELS

Guide students in following these directions to make their models:

1 Color pages 67–68 as desired. Cut out the mini-book page along the outer solid lines. Fold it in half widthwise, and then in half again to make a mini-book.

2 Cut out the spoke-shaped half BASKET pattern on each copy of page 68. Overlap the bases to form a circle and tape.

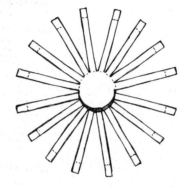

3 Fold down the ends of each of the 16 bands on the basket and tape as shown.

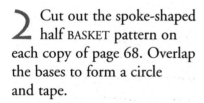

4 Cut out the three long STRIPS on each copy of page 68.

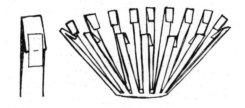

5 Starting at the top of the BASKET, weave one of the STRIPS under the bands as shown. Tape the ends together.

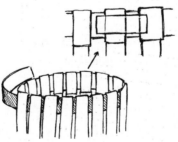

6 Weave the rest of the STRIPS (or with as many as are needed) over and under to complete the BASKET. Apply tape at the end of each strip. Alternate the pattern as shown. Cut off any excess.

TAPE ➡

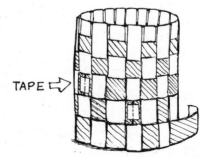

Materials

- ☼ 1 photocopy of page 67 for each student
- ☼ 2 photocopies of page 68 for each student (Enlarge the patterns, if possible.)
- ☼ scissors
- ☼ tape or glue sticks
- ☼ crayons, colored pencils, or markers (optional)

Bring in different kinds of baskets and ask students to do the same. Give them the opportunity to examine the baskets to determine whether they were woven, coiled, twisted, sewn, or made with a combination of methods. Encourage them to study and describe the different patterns woven into the baskets.

TEACHING WITH THE MODELS

1 Why did the Apache make baskets instead of pottery? (*The baskets were more durable than pottery and they were easy to carry from place to place.*)

2 How did the Apache use baskets? (*for carrying and storing food and holding water, as trays, and in ceremonies*)

3 In the Apache tribes, who made baskets? (*the women*)

4 What materials did the weavers use to create their baskets and how did they prepare the materials? (*The weavers gathered reeds or branches, scraped and stripped them, and softened them by submerging them in water or by burying them in sand.*)

5 Challenge students to use their models and mini-books to explain how the weavers made their baskets. (*They wove branches or strips over and under each other to create patterns. They also bundled branches together and then coiled and sewed them into baskets.*) Tell students that although the Apache wove more intricate patterns into their baskets, their model depicts the basic process of Apache basket-making.

2

Basket makers also made coiled baskets by bundling together branches, then coiling and sewing them to form the basket's shape.

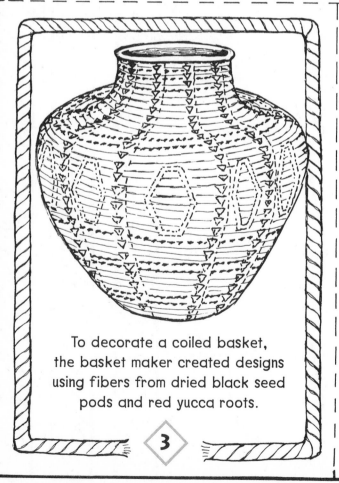

1

To make a twined basket, an Apache woman wove softened branches or reeds in and out of stiffer branches or reeds.

To decorate a coiled basket, the basket maker created designs using fibers from dried black seed pods and red yucca roots.

3

APACHE BASKET-MAKING

WEAVE A BASKET
(APACHE)

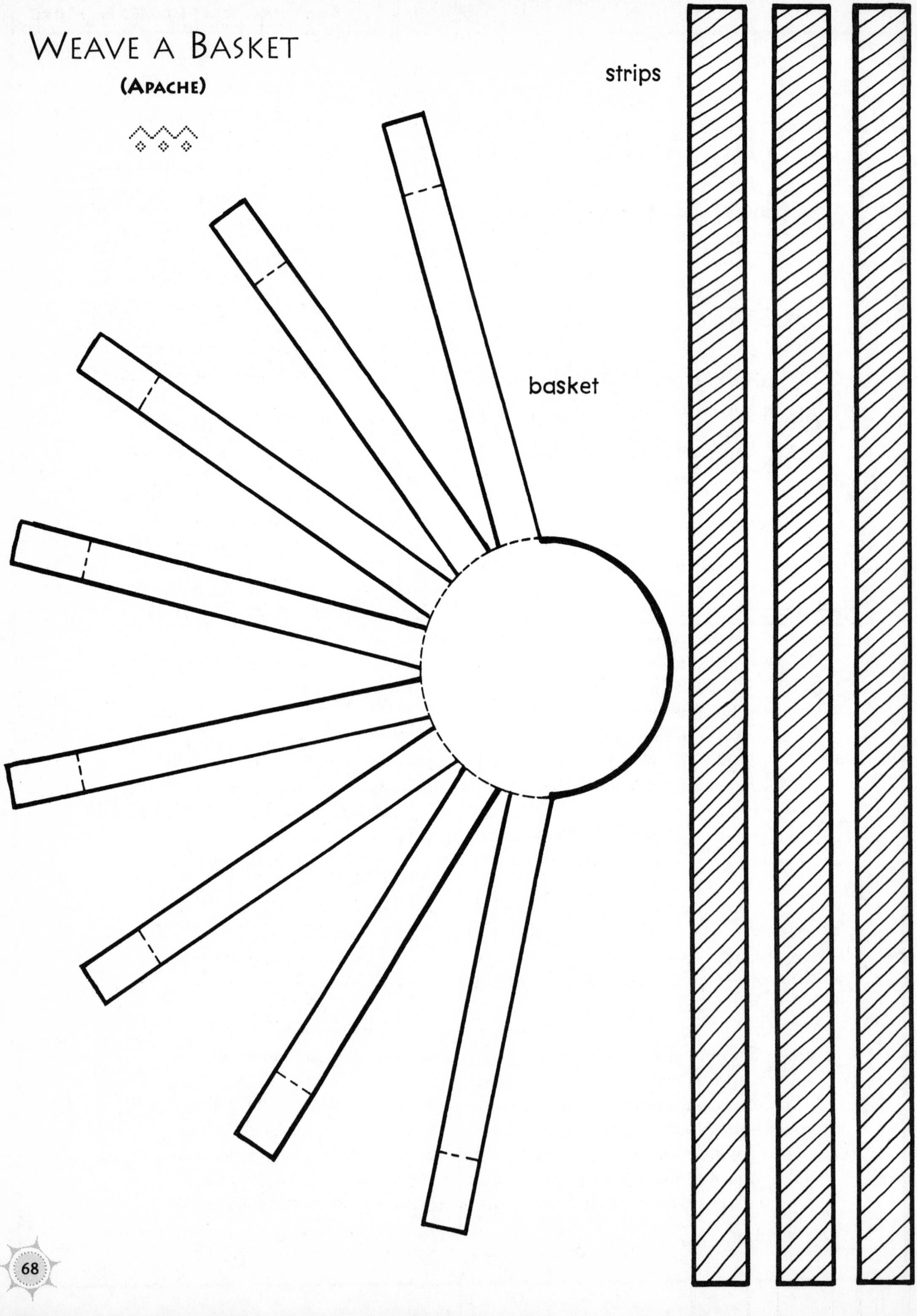

strips

basket

Who Wore What? Double Diorama

(HOPI)

~~~~~~~~

Students make a double diorama that depicts how Hopi men, women, and children dressed.

NATIVE TRADITIONS

The climate in which the Hopi lived was dry most of the year. Temperatures ranged from warm in spring and autumn, to very hot in summer, to quite cold in winter. Even so, the Hopi wore the same kinds of clothing year round. When they had to go outside on windy, cold days, they put on a blanket or a rabbit skin robe for warmth and protection.

The Hopi made their own clothes and moccasins. Men and older boys wore breechcloths of deerskin when working in the fields or hunting. Often they would wear kilt-like woven cotton garments as well. To cover their feet, they wore moccasins made of deerskin. They also wore headbands of cotton or rabbit skin to hold their bangs in place and tied their long hair in a knot at the back of their neck.

In the village, women wore woven cotton dresses that they wrapped around their body, under their left arm, and tied over their right shoulder. Women walked barefoot or wore moccasins. Young children wore little or no clothing and went barefoot. When a girl was ready for marriage she wore her hair in two large whorls that looked like squash blossoms. It could take an hour or more to brush, part, roll, and wind her hair over U-shaped forms made of corn husks or wood.

Both men and women also had deerskin leggings. They wore these for protection from sharp cactus needles, prickly desert shrubs, rocks, and desert animals, such as snakes.

The cotton raised by the Hopi and used to weave cloth for their clothing grew naturally in a variety of colors including rose, brown, rust, pale green, light yellow, and soft purple. They also colored the cloth using dyes made from the pigments in different plants. After Spanish explorers introduced domesticated sheep to the Southwest, the Hopi wove cloth not only from cotton but also from wool.

Materials

☼ photocopies of pages 72–74 for each student

☼ scissors

☼ tape

☼ crayons, colored pencils, or markers (optional)

MAKING THE MODEL

Guide students in following these directions to make their models:

1 Color the pages as desired. Then cut out the two-sided VILLAGE/FIELD pattern on page 72. Fold the pattern in half along the dotted line and tape as shown.

2 Cut out the strips with the HOPI WOMEN and HOPI MEN on pages 73–74. Turn the VILLAGE side so it faces you. Tape one end of the strip with the HOPI WOMEN to each side of the VILLAGE scene as shown. The strip will curve.

3 Repeat step 2 with the FIELD side of the diorama and the strip with the HOPI MEN.

TAPE

4 Cut out the remaining model pieces. Tape each piece (except for the robes) onto its corresponding scene.

TEACHING WITH THE MODEL

1 What did Hopi men wear to work in the fields or to hunt? (*deerskin breechcloths and moccasins, kilt-like cotton garments*)

2 What did Hopi women wear in the village? (*cotton dresses, sometimes moccasins*)

3 When did girls wear their hair in two whorls? (*when they were ready for marriage*)

4 Have students describe the details depicted in each background scene, what each person is wearing, as well as other items in the diorama.

5 Why did the Hopi wear deerskin leggings when they went out of their village? (*to protect them from desert animals, prickly plants, and rocks*)

6 What did the Hopi men wear when the weather was cold? (*They put on blankets or rabbit skin robes.*) Invite students to fold down the tabs on the robes provided and put them on the corresponding people.

The Hopi lived in what is today northeastern Arizona. Challenge students to make a graph of the average monthly temperature in that region over the course of one year. Have them make another graph of monthly rainfall in the same region. To collect their data, direct them to references, such as almanacs, the Internet, and so on. (Always supervise students' use of the Internet.)

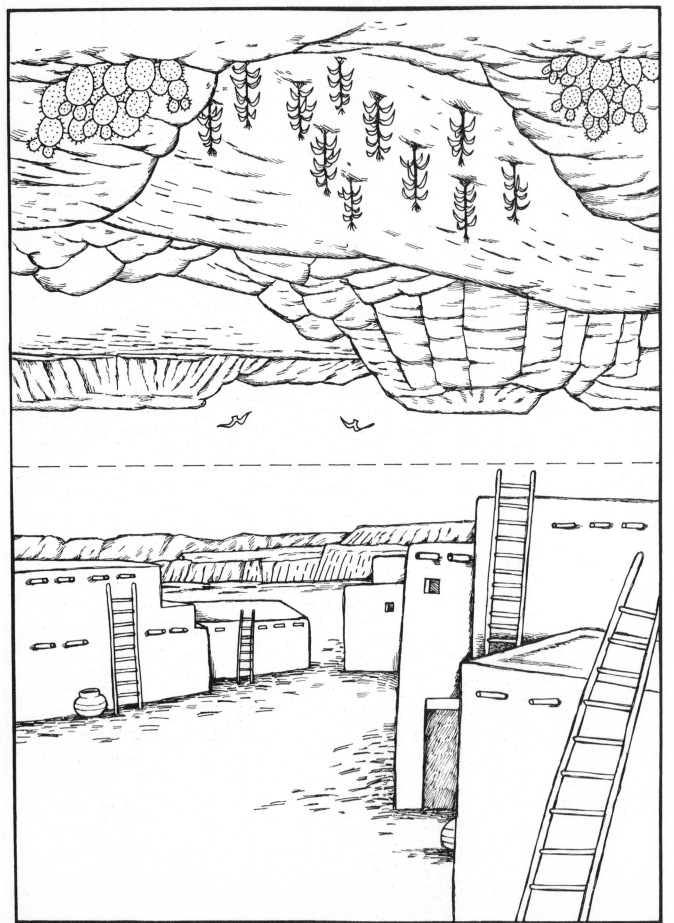

village

Who Wore What?
Double Diorama
(Hopi)

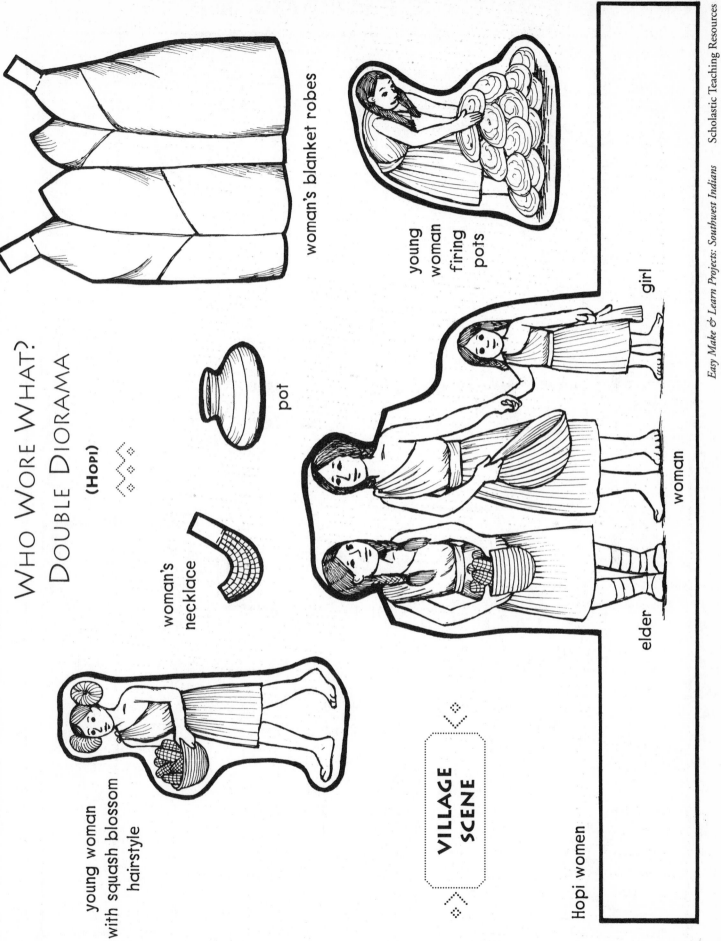

woman's blanket robes

young woman firing pots

pot

woman's necklace

young woman with squash blossom hairstyle

VILLAGE SCENE

Hopi women

elder

woman

girl

Who Wore What? Double Diorama (Hopi)

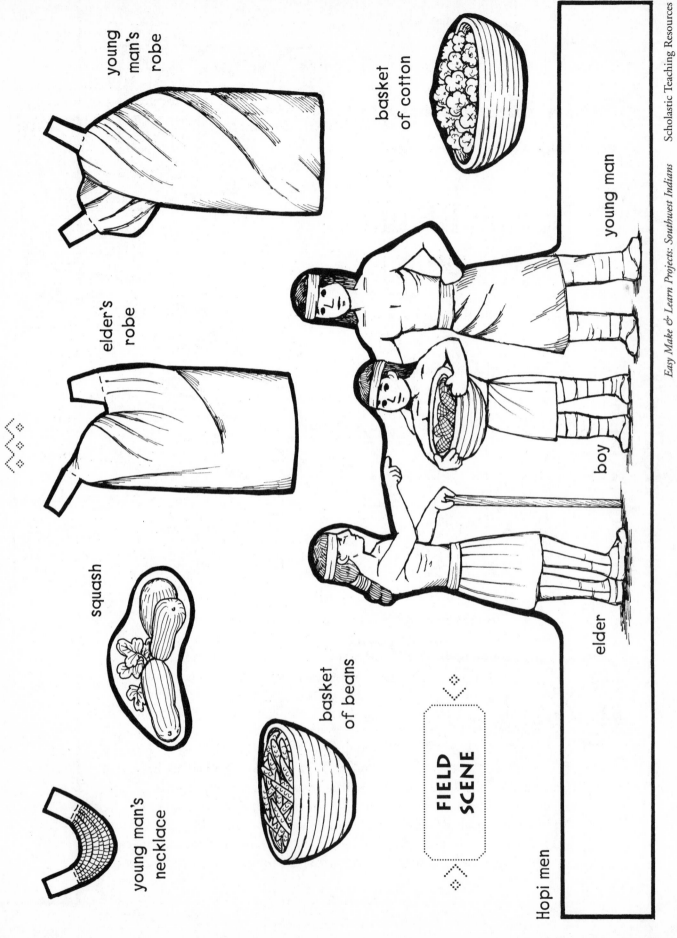

young man's robe

basket of cotton

elder's robe

squash

basket of beans

young man's necklace

FIELD SCENE

Hopi men

elder

boy

young man

Easy Make & Learn Projects: Southwest Indians   Scholastic Teaching Resources

From Sheep to Blanket

Navajo Blankets Mini-Book

(NAVAJO)

Students weave a model of a Navajo blanket and make a mini-book that describes how blankets were made.

NATIVE TRADITIONS

After the Spanish arrived in 1540, they introduced horses, cattle, and domesticated sheep into the Southwest. Over time, the Navajo developed skills in raising livestock for transportation, food, and wool. They became expert horse riders and raised great herds of sheep. Every Navajo child had a lamb to learn about sheep and how to care for them.

In the spring, Navajo men and women used knives made of sharpened stones to shear the wool from their sheep. Women spun the wool into yarn, colored the yarn with plant dyes, and used it to weave beautiful blankets for bedding and clothing. A woman might have had a wooden loom inside her hogan and one outside. She wove from the bottom up, creating designs of stripes, diamonds, zigzags, crosses, and other geometric patterns. When a weaver removed a completed blanket from her loom, it would curl, so she buried it in damp sand for a few days to flatten it. In the late nineteenth century, Navajo women began weaving rugs, which were highly prized and in great demand.

Materials

- photocopies of pages 77–78 for each student
- scissors
- tape
- ten 8-inch strips of different colored paper (for each student)
- crayons, colored pencils, or markers (optional)

Do More!

There is a Navajo legend that explains how Navajo women learned how to weave on a loom. Find a version of the legend, such as *Magic of Spider Woman* retold by Lois Duncan (Scholastic, 1996) or *The Magic Weaver of Rugs: A Tale of the Navajo* retold by Jerrie Oughton (Houghton Mifflin, 1994), and share it with students. Encourage them to write and illustrate a retelling of the legend.

Follow up with a look at the role of weaving in contemporary Navajo culture by sharing *Songs From the Loom: A Navajo Girl Learns to Weave* by Monty Roessel, part of the We Are Still Here: Native Americans Today series (Lerner, 1995).

MAKING THE MODELS

Guide students in following these directions to make their models:

1 Color pages 77–78 as desired. Fold page 77 in half and then in half again to make a mini-book.

2 Gently fold page 78 in half the short way. Starting at the fold, cut all the way along each of the 18 lines on the pattern.

3 Open the paper and spread it flat. Starting at the bottom of the loom, from the back, weave the first strip of paper through the slits, weaving over and under them as shown.

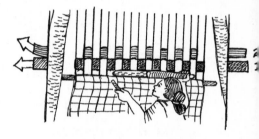

4 Continue weaving strips (alternating colors as well) until you have filled the loom. Push the strips close together as you work.

5 When the weaving is complete, turn the page over. Trim any excess from the ends of the strips and tape down the ends as shown.

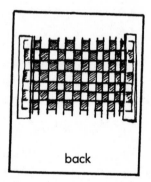

back

TEACHING WITH THE MODELS

1 What kind of livestock did the Navajo raise? How did they use the livestock? (*horses for transportation, sheep for wool and food, cattle for food*)

2 Where did the Navajo get yarn for weaving? (*After the arrival of the Spanish, they raised domesticated sheep, sheared wool from them, spun the yarn from the wool, and colored it with plant dyes.*)

3 What did Navajo women weave? (*They wove blankets for bedding and clothing. Later they also wove rugs.*)

4 Challenge students to use their loom models and mini-books to explain the process used by the Navajo to make blankets. (*They wove yarn over and under on a loom to create patterns, then buried a completed blanket in damp sand to flatten it.*)

2

Using wooden looms, women wove the blankets from the bottom up, creating designs of stripes, diamonds, zigzags, and other geometric patterns.

1

After shearing wool from sheep, Navajo women spun the wool into yarn and then colored it using plant dyes.

3

When taken off the loom, a finished blanket would curl. To flatten it, weavers buried the blanket in damp sand for a few days.

NAVAJO BLANKETS

FROM SHEEP TO BLANKET (NAVAJO)

Resources

BOOKS FOR TEACHERS

America's Fascinating Indian Heritage edited by James A. Maxwell (Reader's Digest, 1990). Covering the major Native culture areas, this beautifully illustrated book is full of information about the history and daily life of Native Americans in the past.

Dancing in the Paths of the Ancestors and *Pueblo People of the Earth Mother* by Thomas E. Mails (Marlowe and Company, 1998, 1999). These comprehensive companion resources on the Pueblo peoples detail their history and their way of life.

A Native American Encyclopedia: History, Culture, and Peoples, Volumes 1 and 2 edited by Barry M. Pritzker (ABC-CLIO, 1998). An authoritative reference that discusses topics such as the history, government, customs, dwellings, diet, and dress of more than 200 Native American groups and provides information about their lives today.

The Native Americans: The Indigenous People of North America, edited by Richard Collins (Salamander Books Ltd., 1999). Fascinating pictures and photographs of tribal artifacts from nine Native American culture areas are a highlight of this book. The book also explores how different groups long ago adapted to a range of environments.

BOOKS FOR STUDENTS

Atlas of Indians of North America by Gilbert Legay (Barron's Educational Series, 1995). This book offers a good introduction to some of the Southwest Indian tribes with illustrations depicting how members of each tribe dressed.

Children of Clay: A Family of Pueblo Potters by Rina Swentzell (Lerner, 1995). This nonfiction book details how a contemporary family from the Santa Clara Pueblo in New Mexico continue the traditional art of making pottery—from collecting the clay in nearby mountains, to shaping and decorating the pots. Part of the We Are Still Here: Native Americans Today series.

The First Americans: The Story of Where They Came From and Who They Became by Anthony F. Aveni (Scholastic, 2005). Beginning with the ancestors of Native Americans who first migrated to North America, this accessible and handsomely illustrated book focuses on five geographic regions and the people who lived there, including the Anasazi of the Southwest, the ancestors of the Pueblo Indians. The book also explores how scientists uncover and make meaning from artifacts of the past.

From Abenaki to Zuni: A Dictionary of Native American Tribes by Evelyn Wolfson (Walker and Company, 1988/1995). Useful as a survey guide to 68 Indian tribes in North America, this resource includes information about major culture areas and language families, as well as brief overviews of each tribe's history, location, customs, housing, and more.

Houses of Adobe by Bonnie Shemie (Tundra Books, 1993). Detailed illustrations paired with easy-to-read text invite readers to learn about and compare different types of architecture, such as cliff dwellings, pueblos, and kivas, built by Southwest Native peoples centuries ago.

...If You Lived With the Hopi by Anne Kamma (Scholastic, 1999). The question-and-answer format of this book serves as a comprehensive introduction to life among the Hopi centuries ago.

Junior Library of American Indian series (Chelsea House, 1992, 1994). Each book in this series focuses on the culture, history, and contemporary life of different tribes. Individual titles about Southwest Indians include: *The Apache Indians* by Nicole Claro and *The Pueblo Indians* by Lisa N. Burby.

Native American Architecture by Peter Nabokov (Oxford University Press, 1989). Though the text is above grade level, the remarkable photographs of Native American homes make this book a worthwhile resource for students.

Native American Rock Art: Messages From the Past by Yvette La Pierre (Hobbs, 1994). The author describes the ways archaeologists find out how early peoples created pictographs and the ways in which they attempt to interpret what they mean.

The Pueblo by Charlotte Yue and David Yue (Houghton Mifflin, 1990). The authors focus on the centuries-old dwellings of Pueblo tribes and include a wealth of information about the daily lives of these peoples. Clear pictures and diagrams accompany the text.

The Scholastic Encyclopedia of the North American Indian by James Ciment, Ph.D. with Ronald LaFrance, Ph.D. (Scholastic, 1996). In this information-packed resource, readers learn about 149 tribal and regional Indian groups.

The Zuni by Edmund J. Ladd (Raintree Steck-Vaughn, 2000). Illustrations, photos, and maps enhance text that focuses on the culture, family life, and history of the Zuni people. There is a discussion of contempor
well as a chronology.

WEB SITES

First Nations Histories

www.tolatsga.org/Compacts.html

Find comprehensive historical information about specific tribes throughout North America here.

The Hopi Tribe: Farming

www.hopi.nsn.us/farming.asp

This page on the official Hopi tribe Web site provides information about traditional and modern-day Hopi farming methods. Other pages on the site (www.hopi.nsn.us) provide concise information about Hopi culture, history, and housing.

Indian Pueblo Cultural Center

www.indianpueblo.org/index.cfm?module=ipcc&pn=15

Includes brief descriptions of the culture, history, arts, and contemporary life of New Mexico's 19 Pueblos.

Indigenous Peoples of New Mexico

www.cybergata.com/native.htm

Visit this site to see photos of pueblos, kivas, and more.

The Language of Native American Baskets From the Weavers' View

www.nmai.si.edu/exhibitions/baskets/
subpage.cfm?subpage=burden

This online exhibition on the Web site of the Smithsonian National Museum of the American Indian explores the traditional use of burden baskets by many Native American cultures and displays a variety of these baskets from different tribes and periods in history.

Native North America

www.mnsu.edu/emuseum/cultural/
northamerica/index.shtml

museum at Minnesota State
features information about the
technologies, and daily life of specific
orth America.